Understanding

The Canterbury Tales

UNDERSTANDING GREAT LITERATURE

Clarice Swisher

LUCENT
BOOKS ®

THOMSON

™

GALE

San Diego • Detroit • New York • San Francisco • Cleveland
New Haven, Conn. • Waterville, Maine • London • Munich

For Alex

On cover: Chaucer's pilgrims make their way to Canterbury.

LIBRARY OF CONGRESS CATALOGING-IN-PUBLICATION DATA

Swisher, Clarice, 1933–
    The Canterbury tales / by Clarice Swisher.
    p. cm. — (Understanding Great Literature)
Summary: Discusses the life of Geoffrey Chaucer and the historical context, plot, themes,
characters, and literary devices of his work *The Canterbury Tales.*
Includes bibliographical references (p.) and index.
    ISBN 1-56006-782-9 (hardback : alk. paper)
    1. Chaucer, Geoffrey, d. 1400. Canterbury tales—Juvenile literature. 2. Christian pilgrims
and pilgrimages in literature—Juvenile literature. 3. Tales, Medieval—History and criticism
—Juvenile literature. 4. Storytelling in literature—Juvenile literature. I. Title. II. Series
    PR1874 .S95 2003
    821' .1—dc21
                                                                          2002155187

Printed in the United States of America

Contents

FOREWORD

"Except for a living man, there is nothing more wonderful than a book!" wrote the widely respected nineteenth-century teacher and writer Charles Kingsley. A book, he continued, "is a message to us from human souls we never saw. And yet these [books] arouse us, terrify us, teach us, comfort us, open our hearts to us as brothers." There are many different kinds of books, of course; and Kingsley was referring mainly to those containing literature—novels, plays, short stories, poems, and so on. In particular, he had in mind those works of literature that were and remain widely popular with readers of all ages and from many walks of life.

Such popularity might be based on one or several factors. On the one hand, a book might be read and studied by people in generation after generation because it is a literary classic, with characters and themes of universal relevance and appeal. Homer's epic poems, the *Iliad* and the *Odyssey*, Chaucer's *Canterbury Tales*, Shakespeare's *Hamlet* and *Romeo and Juliet*, and Dickens's *A Christmas Carol* fall into this category. Some popular books, on the other hand, are more controversial. Mark Twain's *Huckleberry Finn* and J.D. Salinger's *The Catcher in the Rye*, for instance, have their legions of devoted fans who see them as great literature; while others view them as less than worthy because of their racial depictions, profanity, or other factors.

Still another category of popular literature includes realistic modern fiction, including novels such as Robert Cormier's *I Am the Cheese* and S.E. Hinton's *The Outsiders*. Their keen social insights and sharp character portrayals have consistently reached out to and captured the imaginations of many teen-agers and young adults; and for this reason they are often assigned and studied in schools.

These and other similar works have become the "old stan-dards" of the literary scene. They are the ones that people most often read, discuss, and study; and each has, by virtue of its con-tent, critical success, or just plain longevity, earned the right to be the subject of a book examining its content. (Some, of course, like the *Iliad* and *Hamlet*, have been the subjects of numerous books already; but their literary stature is so lofty that there can never be too many books about them!) For millions of readers and students in one generation after another, each of these works becomes, in a sense, an adventure in appreciation, enjoyment, and learning.

The main purpose of Lucent's Understanding Great Literature series is to aid the reader in that ongoing literary adventure. Each volume in the series focuses on a single liter-ary work that a majority of critics and teachers view as a classic and/or that is widely studied and discussed in schools. A typi-cal volume first tells why the work in question is important. Then follow detailed overviews of the author's life, the work's historical background, its plot, its characters, and its themes. Numerous quotes from the work, as well as by critics and other experts, are interspersed throughout and carefully document-ed with footnotes for those who wish to pursue further research. Also included is a list of ideas for essays and other stu-dent projects relating to the work, an appendix of literary criti-cisms and analyses by noted scholars, and a comprehensive annotated bibliography.

The great nineteenth-century American poet Henry David Thoreau once quipped: "Read the best books first, or you may not have a chance to read them at all." For those who are read-ing or about to read the "best books" in the literary canon, the comprehensive, thorough, and thoughtful volumes of the Understanding Great Literature series are indispensable guides and sources of enrichment.

INTRODUCTION

The Canterbury Tales: Chaucer's "Plenty"

*T*he *Canterbury Tales*, Geoffrey Chaucer's triumphant work, has fascinated both ordinary readers and literary scholars for six hundred years. One reason *The Canterbury Tales* has lasted is that Chaucer offers lively portraits and stories that appeal to a diverse audience. There is something for those who like a good story, those who want a good laugh, those interested in history or a debate about moral subjects, and those interested in the historical roots of the English language.

For readers who like a good story, there are romances and tales of hardship overcome. For example, "The Knight's Tale" keeps the reader in suspense waiting to find out who will win a beautiful lady's affections. In "The Clerk's Tale," the reader is kept in wonder at a wife's capacity to endure the abuse meted out by her husband. In her book *Geoffrey Chaucer*, Velma Bourgeois Richmond says, "The brilliance of his story telling assures a good read and an increased thoughtfulness as well as laughter."[1]

For readers who want a good laugh, Chaucer has jokes aplenty. In "The Miller's Tale," the reader can hardly keep from laughing out loud at the image of a foolish carpenter sitting in a tub awaiting a flood. For more subtle humor, Chaucer deliberately writes bad poetry as a means of poking fun at the bumbling knight Sir Topaz.

For serious readers of history, *The Canterbury Tales* provides insights into medieval English society. "The Prologue," for example, offers a portrait gallery of individuals who were familiar figures in medieval England. Readers can glean information on the beliefs and concerns of the English people in those times. For example, in the tales of the wife of Bath and the clerk, Chaucer provides opposing views of marriage; in the tales of the parson and the pardoner, the reader sees two opposing views of what constitutes morality. Other paired and contrasting stories invite readers to contemplate the nature of justice and the importance of social status and rank.

For readers interested in literature as an art form, *The Canterbury Tales* offers plenty indeed. During the years he was writing *The Canterbury Tales,* Chaucer was experimenting with new literary forms. According to literary scholar C. David Benson, "The *Canterbury Tales* is a collection of absolutely different kinds of poetry: each contributes a special artistic vision."[2] There are also numerous questions regarding Chaucer's artistry: how Chaucer structured his work; how he used humor to make a subtle point; what images and themes recur throughout. Bernard F. Huppe says in *A Reading of the "Canterbury Tales"* that Chaucer's work "is high art, and it demands high effort from its readers; to give it less is to betray its greatness as art and its amplitude as a vision of the human comedy of man's tragic pilgrimage."[3]

For these many pleasures, opportunities, and challenges, modern readers will find Chaucer and his pilgrims worthy of their time and effort. As English poet John Dryden said of *The Canterbury Tales* in 1700, "'Tis sufficient to say, according to the proverb, that here is God's plenty."[4]

CHAPTER ONE

The Life of Geoffrey Chaucer

No record of Geoffrey Chaucer's birth has survived, but scholars believe he was born in London in 1341 or 1342. Chaucer's parents, John and Agnes Chaucer, both came from prosperous middle-class families. John Chaucer was a successful wine merchant; Agnes, as was common practice among well-to-do families, stayed at home, overseeing the running of the household.

Chaucer's Childhood

The family's prosperity offered Geoffrey a pleasant childhood. The Chaucers lived in a large, comfortable home on Thames Street, a block from the River Thames. Their dwelling included rooms for John's wine business, living quarters hung with tapestries, a sleeping loft, and a courtyard where chickens ran about and a garden grew.

A nurse, who served Geoffrey's every need, tended him through his first years. In *Chaucer's World,* Edith Rickert quotes a writer of the day who describes the qualities of a child's nurse. She says a nurse is, like as the mother . . . glad if the child be glad, and heavy if the child be sorry. . . . And she cheweth meat in her mouth, and maketh it ready to the toothless child . . . and so she feedeth the child when it is hungered, and pleaseth the child with whispering and songs when it shall sleep, and swatheth it in sweet clothes.[5]

Geoffrey's life, however, was not all calm and quiet. He grew up in the excitement of London, then a city of forty thousand inhabitants. He lived near streets filled with shops

The son of prosperous parents, Geoffrey Chaucer spent much of his childhood in the bustling medieval city of London.

and churches. In *Chaucer: His Life, His Works, His World,* Donald R. Howard describes the London scene:

> By day it was bustling and noisy with its hubbub of iron wagon wheels, peddlers' cries, city dwellers' shouts— and also with what are to us country noises, horses neighing, barnyard clucking, bird songs, the barking of ubiquitous dogs. At night the curfew rang at eight, nine in the summer, and there descended an awesome silence complicated by the rhythms of [church] bells.[6]

The curfew Howard mentions was necessary and universally observed. Thieves and other criminals made their homes just across the river, and anyone who ventured outside the city's walls after the curfew risked being robbed—or worse.

Despite the restrictions on movement at night, life could hardly be described as grim. People found ways of having fun. For example, they attended weekend fairs and athletic competitions. Part of the entertainment was the fighting that often broke out because of the spirited rivalry among competing players.

The scene at home, when families gathered for meals or socialized with friends and relatives, could be similarly lively. The English people of Chaucer's time had a reputation for being noisy and spirited. They tended to be open with their feelings and outspoken in their expression of them. Historian John Gardner notes, "When greeting each other, they hugged and kissed like modern Frenchmen; when insulted or injured they snatched at their daggers without thinking."[7] Parents showered their children with affection and included them in many of their activities, such as visiting shops or going to church.

Chaucer's Education

In spite of the family's contentment in their London home, in 1347 they moved to the port city of Southampton. There,

John Chaucer fulfilled a request that he serve as the king's deputy, responsible for collecting import duties on wine. While in Southampton, Geoffrey began studies with a schoolmaster, who taught the youngster manners, prayers, hymns, and the first lessons in reading and writing Latin.

After two years in Southampton, the Chaucers moved back to London. Geoffrey continued his education, likely at St. Paul's grammar school. Associated with St. Paul's Cathedral, the grammar school was also a song school, a place where young boys were taught to sing in the cathedral choir. Scholars believe, in fact, that a child portrayed in "The Prioress's Tale" may be based on one of the other boys who attended St. Paul's.

Exactly what young Geoffrey studied at grammar school is uncertain, but in his works Chaucer displays familiarity with logic, Latin grammar, and the works of classical Roman writers such as Seneca. The form of his early works and his frequent use of French words are believed to indicate that he studied formal French as well.

Although scholars can guess at which authors Geoffrey read, they are uncertain of the specific works. Still, researchers have concluded, based on Chaucer's later works, that as a youngster he read books contained in a collection owned by a schoolmaster named William Ravenstone. These books, according to Derek Brewer in *A New Introduction to Chaucer,* were "exactly the kind that Chaucer's poetry shows him to have read."[8]

Young Geoffrey's education was likely broader than the formal schooling offered by St. Paul's. He most likely learned arithmetic from his father, whose job would have involved doing basic mathematical calculations. Also, like most people in medieval England, Geoffrey would also have learned the art of storytelling since books were expensive and hard to obtain. Geoffrey would have heard folktales that had been passed down for generations or recitations of the news of the day. Geoffrey also would have heard moralistic stories incorporated into sermons at church. Such stories were drawn from the Bible and from the priest's experiences and were meant to emphasize the consequences of sin.

Chaucer's First Job

Geoffrey attended grammar school for the customary seven years. When he finished this phase of his education, Chaucer was fourteen years old and was considered a man. By this time the dominant aspects of his personality had been established. He was bright and curious and loved books. He liked to watch people and found their faults amusing rather than finding them a reason for blame and judgment. Gardner says, "To Chaucer life was a magnificent affair."[9]

Young men of Chaucer's social class customarily continued their education. Some would study law under a practicing lawyer; others might attend a university to study philosophy or theology. An appointment to serve the royal family, which also afforded a young man the chance for further education, was also an option, and it was this path that Chaucer took. Through connections his father had developed, Geoffrey Chaucer received an appointment to work in the castle of the earl and countess of Ulster, Prince Lionel and his wife, Elizabeth. Lionel's father was England's ruler, King Edward III. Court records show that on April 4, 1357, a tunic (a long shirt) and hose were purchased for the young Chaucer to wear in his job as a page.

Pages were expected to make themselves useful and behave themselves. Howard explains the rules provided in the courtesy books for pages:

> Don't quarrel, don't point, don't whisper, don't speak improperly to women, don't tell lies, don't scratch or make faces or yawn, don't pick your nose or blow it too loud, spit too far, belch, "fire your rear guns," pick your teeth, gape, pout. . . . Some of the dont's (don't

As a young man, Chaucer became the page of Prince Lionel. Here, a page carries a basket of fruit.

blow your nose on your napkin, don't wipe your teeth on the tablecloth) are fairly ludicrous and might have been included as jokes.[10]

People and Experiences in Lionel's Court

While at Lionel's court, Chaucer met other members of the royal family. He even met the king at one of the family feasts. At the 1357 Christmas festivities, Chaucer also met Lionel's younger brother, John of Gaunt, earl of Richmond. Gaunt was seventeen and the family intellectual, who sought friends among philosophers, theologians, and political theorists. Chaucer had already exhibited his wit and learning at court, because Gaunt sought him out. Because they shared similar intellectual interests, Gaunt and Chaucer became friends

13

immediately. Gaunt became Chaucer's patron, arranging for yearly grants of money. From that time on, Chaucer was a staunch supporter of the royal family. When Gaunt married the duke of Lancaster's daughter, Blanche, in 1359, Chaucer became friends with her as well.

Courtiers like Chaucer were expected to do whatever the royal family wished, regardless of their training. Therefore, in 1359, when England mounted an invasion of France with the goal of capturing Paris, Chaucer accepted his assignment to a knight (perhaps Lionel himself) on the expedition. In this capacity, he fulfilled tasks such as carrying lances, lighting fires, dressing his master and other knights in their armor, hunting and scavenging for food—which meant engaging in the common practice of looting the homes of peasants. On March 1, 1360, on one of his errands, Chaucer was captured by the French. Because Chaucer was a loyal and valued servant of the royal family, Edward III paid a ransom of £16 (or about $3,840) to free him. Meanwhile, the English army marched toward Paris, but before the English could actually attack, a violent hailstorm struck. The invasion stalled altogether, and eventually the two sides agreed to peace. Chaucer and the army were home by May 1360.

Chaucer's Court Education

No records have been found of Chaucer's activities from the time of his return to England in 1360 until 1367, but historians have pieced together circumstantial evidence. They believe that Chaucer continued to serve the royal court, either in Lionel's court or in the court of his older brother Edward, known as the Black Prince. At court, Chaucer had the chance to observe and mimic the behavior of the nobility, an opportunity that most members of merchant-class families never got. As Howard writes, Chaucer was able "to learn the niceties of highborn conduct and the arts of war—to learn how things were done among the nobles and royals."[11]

While serving in court, historians believe, Chaucer probably continued his education in the form of tutoring by learned visitors from both England and Europe. Furthermore, scholars of various disciplines were always in residence and were generally willing to share their learning with those who expressed an interest. In this way, Chaucer achieved a technical knowledge of law and a working knowledge of many subjects.

By this time, Chaucer knew he wanted to be a poet and had many opportunities to write poetry for the court and to recite his poems publicly. To further his goal, Chaucer studied whatever disciplines he could. According to Gardner:

> Chaucer felt he had no choice, if he wished to be a first-rate poet, but to pursue by whatever means available what we might call, loosely, metaphysics, the interrelationship of form and matter, higher and lower living orders (from worms to angels to Platonic spirits), geometry, numerology, astrology, alchemy [a medieval chemical philosophy], the philosophy of music, and so on.[12]

In his position as courtier, Chaucer was expected to be a court entertainer, and he chose to be a poetic apprentice, a person in training to write poetry to be read aloud for entertainment. To advance his court position, Chaucer also needed to continue his study of French and Latin. Although Parliament had made English the official national language in 1362, only gradually did English become the language of the court. French was still the language most spoken at court and Latin was the language used by scholars.

Chaucer's Family Matters

By 1367 Chaucer was working in the household of King Edward and Queen Philippa; a year later he was known as "esquire," a title that connoted rank. During this time Chaucer married Philippa Roet, who worked as lady-in-waiting to the queen. The

King Edward III (pictured) employed Chaucer in 1367. The poet held a number of important positions under the king.

Chaucers had three children: Katherine, Thomas, and Lewis.

Philippa Chaucer had royal connections of her own: Her sister Katherine was lady-in-waiting to the wife of Chaucer's old friend John of Gaunt. Katherine was also Gaunt's mistress. Then, when Gaunt's wife, Constance, died in 1396, Gaunt married Katherine. By this means, Chaucer and Gaunt became brothers-in-law. This development worked to the Chaucers' benefit. Records show numerous grants from John of Gaunt to both Geoffrey and Philippa Chaucer. Howard sums up what this connection meant for Chaucer, noting, "What must be remembered is that Chaucer *married well,* and the marriage brought him advantages of status, connections, and annuities."[13]

Chaucer as Public Servant and Writer

In the service of the royal family, Chaucer undertook sensitive foreign assignments, many of which required diplomatic skills. For example, Chaucer negotiated an agreement to keep the Spanish navy from coming under French control, another treaty securing docking rights for English ships in Genoa, and an effort, though unsuccessful, to negotiate with French nobility for a wife for Richard, Edward's grandson. Chaucer used each of these diplomatic assignments to add to his education and to learn about the art and literature of whatever city or country he was visiting.

Chaucer's domestic duties expanded in June 1374, when the king appointed Chaucer to the important post of controller of customs, a job that managed the import fees to be paid to the treasury. In this job, which he held for twelve years, he was assigned to the port of London to keep handwritten records of customs fees and to supervise two other workers. Brewer comments on Chaucer's work: "There is every reason to suppose Chaucer high in favour at court, and regarded as an accomplished courtier, diplomat and administrator."[14]

At the same time, Chaucer was developing his skills as a poet. Much of his literary effort involved studying French court poets and translating their works into English. This period of Chaucer's writing is called his French period. He learned how to write poems of courtly love, how to create allegory, and how to use the technique of the dream vision. His most important poem from this period is *The Book of the Duchess,* which incorporates all of the techniques he had learned from reading the works of French writers.

Chaucer Is Influenced by Italian Culture

At this point, however, writing was still an avocation for Chaucer, as he continued to represent the king in foreign lands. Eventually, when his travels took him again to Italy, Chaucer's work intersected his art. Howard explains how an official trip to Italy gave Chaucer new insights:

> Chaucer had seen what was undeniably a superior culture: Italy, in his day, led Europe in the arts of civilization. It had the largest, most commercially powerful cities, a new and seemingly effective form of city government; it led Europe in medicine, in scholarship, in art; it was the center of banking and finance. It had a new spirit in literature, and a literary culture unlike anything anywhere in Europe.[15]

Chaucer also noticed that in Italy ordinary people read literature written in the language they spoke. In England, by contrast, literate people from the nobility read mostly Latin or

17

French; most ordinary people had no literature written in the English they spoke. Chaucer was also struck by the humane attitude Italian artists displayed toward their subjects. Gardner explains:

> Wherever he went in Florence [Italy], Chaucer saw frescoes [wall paintings], paintings, and sculptures that celebrated humanness: man's warts, the roughness of his elbows, the distortion of his shoulders when he walked with a Bible clamped under one arm, and also man's inclination toward nobility and goodness.[16]

Chaucer also became acquainted with the work of Italian poets. Howard says, "The influence of Italian literature on Chaucer's writings came not immediately upon his reading

Dante Alighieri, author of The Divine Comedy, *was one of several Italian poets who influenced Chaucer's work.*

the books, but slowly, after being there in Florence . . . and in the interim reading and rereading them."[17] Other Italian writers, such as Dante and Giovanni Boccaccio would also have a noticeable effect on Chaucer's work. A third Italian writer, Petrarch, would influence Chaucer's overall attitude toward his own work. As a poet, Petrarch enjoyed power and fame in Italian society. According to Howard, Chaucer was impressed by Petrarch's status and imagined that "like the 'glory' knights won for deeds of arms, the poet could lay claim to his share of worldly luster."[18]

Chaucer's Honors and Income Opportunities

Chaucer's success as a traveling diplomat brought him honors and rewards at court, as did his poetry. Chaucer was no longer a poet apprentice but a star poet. As such, the court considered him a symbol of status. Gardner says, "Chaucer was an intellectual ornament of the court, one of those government treasures, so to speak, that proved the court's worth and class."[19] For reading a poem at court in 1374, he was granted a pitcher of wine (probably a gallon) per day for the rest of his life. For his work as a diplomat, he was given the right to live rent-free for life in Aldgate, a house built above one of the London gates. As an additional token of appreciation, the king had an elegant red robe made for Chaucer. With these grants, the income from his job as controller, and his annual pension from Gaunt, Chaucer could support himself and his family very well.

Nevertheless, Chaucer found additional ways to make money. He added the oversight of additional functions at the customs office, and he became ward for the estates of Edmund Staplegate and William Soles of Kent. This job as ward entailed keeping up the properties, collecting rents, paying wages of servants, and managing the accounts. With this additional money, he bought a house in Kent. He also bought books. Chaucer accumulated a library of sixty volumes, which he read and thought about. Such a collection represented a substantial investment. Howard says that they "were all copied by hand, the best on vellum [a fine parchment made from calfskin or lambskin] gorgeously illuminated [decorated with ornamental designs] and bound. . . . All books were rare and precious: it is said a good book on vellum would have cost as much as a burgher's house."[20] For Chaucer, however, the value of his collection went far beyond the monetary investment. These were books that represented ideas and knowledge; these were books that he would read and reread.

Changes in Court and Turmoil in London

Just as Chaucer was looking to find peace and quiet and to enjoy his books, the court went through changes and turmoil. When Edward III weakened during a three-year period of illness, there were uprisings in England and outbreaks of war in France. King Edward's son Edward, the Black Prince, was also too sick to rule effectively in his father's stead. When Edward III died on June 26, 1377, his grandson, ten-year-old Richard, was crowned king. The young king was bolstered by administrative assistance from Gaunt and others, but unrest continued. The court levied additional taxes on the peasants, who resented this increased financial burden. As a consequence, in 1381 they revolted and stormed London in what came to be called the Peasant's Revolt.

The new king managed to quell the unrest. Meanwhile, Chaucer maintained his favored position at court, despite the chaos. Furthermore, events offered Chaucer yet another way to serve the king. The time had come to arrange for Richard's marriage. Coincidentally, an unsolicited proposal came from Bohemia suggesting an alliance with England involving the marriage of the Bohemian princess Anne to Richard. Chaucer and the other negotiators studied the proposal and approved it; then on January 14, 1382, Richard married Anne. Both Richard and his new queen liked Chaucer, with the result that

Despite the turmoil caused by the Peasant's Revolt of 1381 (pictured), Chaucer continued to enjoy favor in the royal court.

Chaucer was drawn even closer to the inner circle of Richard's court than he had been in Edward's.

In Service to Richard

While in service to Richard, Chaucer came into his own as a mature writer. He had digested the new techniques and ideas he had learned from Italian writers and modified them to suit his poetry, which he wrote in English. Because of the influence of Italian writers on Chaucer's work during this time, this period is called Chaucer's Italian period. He produced two poems that were adaptations of words by the Italian poet Boccaccio. During this time he also wrote *Parliament of Fowls*. This poem is a dream vision in which birds debate about love. The poem is really an allegory satirizing the English House of Commons. During this period, Chaucer also wrote *Troilus and Criseyde,* the work he considered his best. This work, which took Chaucer six years to write, is the story of two lovers from Greek mythology. As the court poet, Chaucer read these stories aloud to court audiences; they were particularly well received and increased his status and popularity as a poet.

Because he performed admirably in all the tasks asked of him, Chaucer was sought after to perform additional public duties. In Richard's court, Chaucer was made an attendant to Queen Anne, whom he liked because she was educated and liked poetry. Then, on October 12, 1385, he was appointed a justice of peace in Kent. While living in Kent, Chaucer was also elected to Parliament in 1386, and he saw firsthand the workings of the House of Commons. That same year he quit his controller job, but then Richard appointed him clerk of the king's works, which involved managing the care and maintenance of all the king's properties. Chaucer had to travel throughout England, often carrying large sums of money. On his return from one of these trips, he was robbed, slightly injured, and left without his horse. Howard explains Chaucer's dissatisfaction with this job:

> When he reached this height he didn't like the work, or the danger, or the tedium. . . . Traveling about hiring and paying stonemasons and carpenters and laborers, being robbed and beaten up by gangs of highwaymen and left without a horse to find safety, testifying at the numerous trials of the tawdry underworld characters—all that was a different story.[21]

In 1391, at his request, Chaucer was relieved of the clerk's post and instead became the sub-forester in charge of the king's wooded lands.

Chaucer's Last Decades

Despite his numerous public service assignments, Chaucer was able to write more poetry than in earlier times. During this period, encompassing the 1380s and 1390s, called by scholars his English period, Chaucer mapped out and wrote *The Canterbury Tales*. Chaucer wanted to create a collection of tales, mostly written in verse, that were in some way linked together to form a unified work. The device he settled on was what scholars call a frame story. Chaucer's frame is the story of a group of pilgrims on horseback from London to Canterbury. The group sets out from the Tabard Inn, but the night before they depart, the owner of the inn proposes a contest. Each pilgrim is to tell two stories on the way to Canterbury and two on the way back. The host volunteers to guide the trip and judge the stories; the winner is to receive a free dinner at the Tabard Inn. The stories the pilgrims tell are those

Chaucer outlived his wife and many friends from court. His final years, when he wrote The Canterbury Tales, *were his most prolific.*

that Chaucer collected. Chaucer narrates each tale as if he were a reporter, a tactic that gives him license to tell popular bawdy tales that he would never have been allowed to publish otherwise.

This period in Chaucer's life was personally challenging. For example, his wife, Philippa, died in 1387. Gardner says, "Like other good medieval men, he wept and buried her and walked in the fields with his sons."[22] In 1394 three women Chaucer knew well from his work in court died within a few months: Gaunt's second wife, Constance; Mary, wife of Henry, Gaunt's oldest son; and Queen Anne. In 1399 his good friend Gaunt died, and in February 1400 Richard died. Through all of his grief, Chaucer kept writing, as if he knew his time was limited.

As Chaucer neared his own end, he did not endure old age gracefully. He became gloomy and preoccupied with his deteriorating sight and other physical complaints. He thought of old age as a sickness itself. During his last years, he lived in an apartment next to Westminster Abbey. He did, however, write until the very end, when he handed his quill to his son Lewis, uttered his last words, "Farewel my bok and my devocioun!"[23] (Farewell my book and my devotion), and died. He died on October 25, 1400, and was buried in the Poet's Corner in Westminster Abbey.

Clearly, Chaucer stands apart as a writer in medieval times. Gardner says of Chaucer:

> No poet in the whole of English literary tradition, not even Shakespeare, is more appealing, either as a man or as an artist, than Geoffrey Chaucer, or more worthy of biography. . . . Despite the complexity of the philosophical systems and social mores that shaped his thought, Chaucer's general way of looking at things seems clear as an English April day.[24]

CHAPTER TWO

Historical Background

When Chaucer wrote *The Canterbury Tales* during the late fourteenth century, England was undergoing gradual changes in social institutions that had been in existence for almost three hundred years. Chaucer was fully aware of these changes, and in subtle ways he portrays the need for them in *The Canterbury Tales*. For this reason, grasping how people lived in England during the Middle Ages and understanding some of the social trends enhances an appreciation of Chaucer's work.

A Feudal Society

England during the Middle Ages was a feudal society. Feudalism was both a political and an economic system that together imposed tight control on the people. Under feudalism, most people had few opportunities to participate in the decisions that affected their lives. Moreover, few had any opportunity to change their way of life.

As a governing system, feudalism resembled a pyramid. At the top was the king, who, in theory, had absolute power and owned all of the land. Beneath the king were the nobles, to whom the king distributed large tracts of land as a sort of payment for their loyalty. The nobles were supposed to be subordinate to the king, but in practice they held considerable power, thanks to the great wealth they could amass. Beneath the nobles were layers of lesser nobles; each layer was allotted land and in turn distributed that land to still others. This system of division of land into smaller and smaller plots of land repeated until peasants received a few acres—enough land, perhaps, to grow the crops on which they fed their families. Under such a system, virtually everyone owed loyalty to someone else. For all its imperfections, this system—at the beginning, at least—brought order to a chaotic society.

Feudalism was a system for organizing society, but it was also the means by which wealth was generated. The property granted to a nobleman was known as a manor, and it was the major source of the noble's income. In exchange for his land and a cottage, the lord required each peasant to work a certain number of days each year for no pay. The crops the peasants grew were the nobleman's to sell. The lord also collected a tax, called a taille, on the grain, livestock, and chickens the peasant raised on his own little plot of land; he also charged the peasant tolls to have his grain ground at the manor mill and his bread baked in the manor ovens.

The Lord and His Vassal

The size of a manor was measured in fiefs—a unit of land supposedly large enough to support one of the lord's vassals—usually a knight. The number of vassals depended on the wealth of the lord. The primary obligation for the vassal was military service. The vassal's job was to see that the lord's property was protected, and when the lord waged war, the vassal was expected to provide the manpower to do so. This contract between lord and vassal was not one way, however, and imposed requirements on the lord as well. For example, the lord was obligated to protect the vassal from enemies and to ensure that he was treated justly in feudal court should he ever have to appear. The lord could build no castles on the

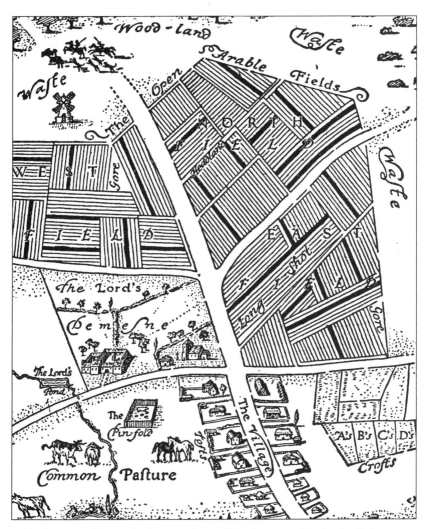

This diagram depicts the layout of a medieval manor. Under feudalism, peasants worked the lands surrounding the lord's manor.

vassal's fief without the vassal's consent. Moreover, the lord pledged to refrain from injuring the vassal's honor by abusing his children or wife.

Chivalry and Knighthood

As the two-way nature of the relationship between the lord and vassal suggests, it was a compact called chivalry. The

27

chivalric ideal provided a code of conduct observed across much of English society. Chivalry was rooted in personal honor and the disgrace one experienced for failing to live up to one's obligations. By Chaucer's time, the chivalric ideal had provided a model for behavior for three hundred years. People knew their places and their responsibilities. An overlord honored his responsibility to provide reasonable protection and living conditions for his vassals and serfs. A serf knew his place and fulfilled his obligations to his lord.

Nobody embodied the chivalric ideal more than the knight, and feudal society depended on knights to uphold the values of chivalry. A knight had to be faithful to his lord and the vows he had taken. He had to be courteous at all

A squire kneels before his king to be knighted. Only after years of training could a squire be made a knight.

times. He vowed to revere womanhood and pledged to protect women, children, and the weak. He performed service to God by protecting the church against enemies and by warring against nonbelievers and heretics.

Training for knighthood took many years. At seven, a young boy went to the house of a nobleman to learn the workings of the castle. At fifteen or sixteen, he became a squire and participated in rigorous training to be a knight, learning to care for horses and equipment and to fight. In *Civilization Past and Present,* T. Walter Wallbank and Alastair M. Taylor describe a squire's training:

> He learned to keep a knight's equipment in good order, to ride a horse with dexterity, and to handle the sword, the shield, and the lance correctly. To that end he practiced long hours in the tilting field against other squires or rode at full gallop against the quintain, an object which administered the passing squire a crushing blow unless it was struck fairly with the lance.[25]

Finally, at twenty-one, the squire was eligible to become a knight. When he had passed the tests of his skills, he was made a knight in an elaborate ceremony.

Attitudes Toward Women

The knight's responsibility for upholding womanhood was clear, yet in medieval society two contrasting attitudes toward women coexisted. Much of the chivalric code was based on the idea that women were made in the image of the Virgin Mary, mother of Jesus. Such women were worthy of being treated with reverence and loyalty, although they were expected to be subservient to their husbands. The other view of women was based on the image of Eve, the biblical temptress who persuaded Adam to eat forbidden fruit and therefore caused humankind to be expelled from the Garden of Eden. According to this view, women used their sexual wiles to tempt men from a virtuous life; they could not be trusted, nor were they entitled to be treated with respect.

In reality, most medieval women experienced neither extreme of treatment. Still, women were hardly free, particularly when it came to marital arrangements. Since women were not allowed an education or an opportunity to earn money, their only choice was to marry, but marriages in all classes were based on practical considerations, not on love. As Bernard D. Grebanier and the editors of *English Literature and Its Backgrounds* explain, "In feudal society marriage was too much bound up with matters of property to be concerned with love; among the nobility it was an affair of business. Moreover, the medieval Church was not interested in encouraging romantic passion."[26] Wives in these marriages, however, made valuable contributions to the relationship, and many marriages resulted in love. Since nobleman were often away from home fighting wars, their wives learned to be effective administrators of large estates. Peasant wives, meanwhile, worked as hard as men in the fields and managed the household and the children as well.

The Power of the Church

The feudal system that the knight helped support was one of two pillars of power; the church was the other. The church was organized in a hierarchy similar to that of feudal society. At the top of the order was the pope. Cardinals, archbishops, bishops, and parish priests made up the remainder of the hierarchy. The church aimed to control people's behavior by a combination of promised rewards and threatened punishments. Grebanier indicates how powerful this combination was:

> From his [an Englishman's] first breath to his dying gasp religion permeated his existence, constantly reminding him not only of the rewards of virtue and the

In feudal society, church officials wielded immense power. Here, the vast hierarchy of the medieval church is depicted, with the pope at center.

awful punishments for sin but also of the undeniable power of ecclesiastical authority. The building of great cathedrals, the founding of the universities at Oxford and Cambridge, the vast waves of crusaders which swept across Europe to the Holy Land—these are obvious examples of the all-pervading influence of the Church in the Middle Ages.[27]

Besides the church's administrative officials and the parish clergy, there were those devoted to spirituality, charity, and learning. Monks, who devoted their lives to religious study and prayer, took rigorous vows and lived cloistered lives in monasteries; nuns, who served the church in similar capacities, lived in convents. Friars also took rigorous vows, but they were sent from the monasteries into the communities to do charitable work. Others gave up worldly goods and devoted themselves to scholarship.

Town Dwellers

By the end of the 1300s, the feudal system that bound most peasants to the land was beginning to decline. Though it was hard to acquire the means to support themselves away from the manor, many serfs were managing to do just that. When a serf had lived in a town for a year and a day, he was considered a free man.

The conditions under which these newly liberated serfs lived could hardly be called ideal. The narrow streets were crowded and there was neither public water nor public sanitation. Animals were everywhere—horses, oxen, pigs, dogs, and geese. Still, people gravitated toward the growing cities. By 1400 London had forty thousand residents. The new arrivals were part of the common people's movement for change. In *The Reformation: A History of European Civilization from Wyclif to Calvin: 1300–1564,* Will Durant explains:

> Those peasants who were still serfs demanded freedom; those who were free called for an end to feudal dues still required of them; and tenants urged that the rent of land should be lowered to four pence ($1.67) per acre per year. Some towns were still subject to feudal overlords, and longed for self-government.[28]

Most of the new town dwellers were craftsmen or merchants. Serfs took the skills they had acquired on the manor and worked in the city as independent craftsmen. Others engaged in buying goods and products and marketing them locally. In this way, the craftsmen and merchants developed a trading economy.

The serf who had gained his freedom was not entirely on his own in the town. Both craftsmen and merchants joined guilds, which were organized to protect workers and enforce

Medieval glassblowers fire and shape their wares. Craftsmen formed the basis of the medieval town economy.

fair business practices. For each trade, such as weaving, tanning, and arrow making, there was a guild that oversaw the work of its members. Pilgrims in *The Canterbury Tales*, such as the haberdasher, dyer, carpenter, weaver, and carpet maker would have belonged to their separate craft guilds; the

33

merchant on the pilgrimage would have belonged to the merchant's guild.

Clear Signs of Decline

Just as feudalism was in decline when Chaucer was writing *The Canterbury Tales,* so too was the church—at least as an unassailable monolith. Preoccupation with wealth among high-level church officials encouraged local friars and other members of the clergy to line their pockets as well. Ordinary people could see this corruption and were increasingly willing to make their objections public. No longer were monks who violated their vow of poverty or other church officials who violated their vow of chastity immune from criticism. Overall, men and women of the church who were guilty of hypocrisy were more likely to be objects of public scorn than they would have been in times past.

Underlying the decline in both the feudal system and the church were repeated epidemics of plague, what was known as the Black Death. Plague first arrived in England in 1348, and epidemics recurred in 1361, 1368, 1375, 1382, and 1390. The Black Death was virtually 100 percent fatal to those infected. Plague killed a third of the total English population, and a thousand villages were essentially wiped out.

The people responded to these terrible and frightening epidemics in a variety of ways. Many thought that God had power over the plague. Starting from this assumption, some people believed that God had deserted them for some reason. Some came to believe that their reliance on prayers and priests had been misguided; others, however, went on pilgrimages to holy sites in hopes that God would notice their faithfulness and spare their lives.

In the countryside, the plague killed so many people that a labor shortage resulted on manors. With workers in short supply, serfs could bargain for wages and for better working conditions. Since feudalism depended on serfs' alliance to

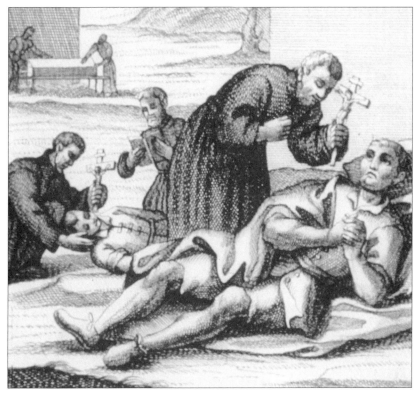

Friars tend to victims of the Black Death, which killed more than one-third of the population of England.

their lords in return for their protection, this empowerment of the people at the bottom contributed to the collapse of the entire system.

The Peasant's Revolt and General Lawlessness

Even as the plague was undermining the feudal system by freeing serfs, a growing dissatisfaction with the taxes levied on them to help pay for wars was creating unrest. In 1381 that dissatisfaction fostered open rebellion. A new tax touched off rioting among peasants in Kent on June 6. Riots spread to other towns and finally peasants stormed the Tower of London and demanded the execution of the officials who had decreed the tax in the king's name. King Richard, now fourteen,

The leader of the Peasant's Revolt is struck down. The insurrection set off an extended period of lawlessness throughout England.

put down the rebellion, but not before rebels had destroyed property throughout the countryside and had burned buildings in London.

Meanwhile, England was in the grip of a crime wave. England had laws to protect its citizens against theft, robbery, and murder, among other crimes. In an effort to maintain control, the aristocracy meted out severe punishments, such as public hangings and beheadings, on those convicted, but crime continued. Gardner describes the conditions:

> For all the care of English law, and for all the high-mindedness of English guildsmen (who were, after all, protecting their own interests in their attempt to keep up quality), crookedness and violence were standard in the Christian Middle Ages. The more ferocious the punishment, the more ingenious the crooks. . . . All

poets agree, and so do the surviving court records, on the darkness and closeness of the con artists' shops or the underground dens of alchemists and "jugglers" (conjurers) and on the danger of alleyways and even main streets after curfew rang, where men were murdered for trifling reasons or no reason at all, stabbed by daggers, run over by horsemen, smashed to the ground by a quarter staff or doorbar in an argument over (in one recorded case) ten apples, or robbed and beaten by midnight roisterers in animal masks.[29]

In numerous ways, *The Canterbury Tales* reflects the times in which Chaucer lived. Chaucer, however, was not a historian but an artist. Yet the art he created captures the essence and truth of his times.

CHAPTER THREE

The Cast
of Characters

The twenty-nine pilgrims in *The Canterbury Tales,* accompanied by the narrator and the host of the Tabard Inn, represent a cross-section of midlevel English society. None of the pilgrims comes from the nobility, nor are there any peasants. The pilgrims on this journey form a company, a fellowship, made up exclusively of English commoners. In his prologue, Chaucer focuses on the appearance, rank, and profession of each pilgrim, suggesting that he meant for each pilgrim to be representative of his or her ilk. However, Chaucer also develops the personality and moral traits of some of the pilgrims, suggesting that he meant for them to be seen as individual characters as well. Donald R. Howard explains that Chaucer, acknowledging the ideal that clearly defined social classes promote societal harmony, "arranged these groups in a sequence from high to low, divided symmetrically by the ideal portraits. First are the Knight and his small retinue."[30]

The Knight
The knight has shed his armor and travels in his sweaty battle clothes, but he rides a fine horse. He follows the chivalric ideal, upholding values such as truth, honor, generosity, and

courtesy. Although he has fought honorably in fifteen battles for Christiandom in many places, such as Russia, Granada, and North Africa, he is still modest. He is also wise and gentle. The knight embodies the qualities of an ideal crusader.

The Squire

The squire, an apprentice learning to be a knight, is in this case the knight's son. A strong man about twenty, he has curly hair, wears red and white flowers, and sings. He is agile and has fought with the cavalry in Flanders. Chaucer says he is a lover who gets little sleep. Chaucer also mentions that he carves his father's meat, in keeping with the squire's position lower in the social order than a knight.

The Yeoman

The yeoman, an independent farmer, serves as the servant for the knight and the squire. Dressed in a green coat and hood, he is a forester carrying a bow and a quiver filled with arrows. Chaucer says the yeoman is skilled in woodcraft. He wears a shiny silver St. Christopher medal for his own good luck as well as a sword, buckler (shield), and dagger, perhaps the knight's war implements. Setting the yeoman apart in this company is the fact that Chaucer depicts only two other pilgrims as carrying weapons or wearing ornaments.

The Prioress

A prioress is a nun who is in charge of a convent. Named Eglantyne, this prioress is more worldly than religious and imitates the nobility in her mannerisms and in her use of French. Her manners are dainty and careful to the extreme; for example, she never drops even the tiniest speck on her breast and wipes her mouth so carefully no one would ever see grease on her lips. She dotes over her dogs and feeds them roast meat and sentimentally weeps over a trapped mouse. She is a large woman wearing a bracelet, a rosary, and a golden brooch. Author Kemp Malone, who suggests that Chaucer is poking gentle fun of the prioress, says, "Chaucer's description of her is the most delicately, daintily humorous passage in the *Canterbury Tales*."[31]

The Second Nun and the Three Priests

The second nun is the prioress's secretary, and she rides with her boss. The three priests also ride with the prioress. Chaucer provides no descriptions of them.

The Monk

Like the prioress, the monk is more worldly than religious. Socially, the monk is one of the highest-ranking pilgrims; he comes from an aristocratic family and lives on his inheritance, even though monks traditionally are supposed to give up wealth and worldly pleasures for a cloistered, spiritual existence. He prefers hunting hares in the field and rejects the idea that a monk must pray in the cloister to be a good monk. He owns many greyhounds and fine horses, wears fur on his sleeves, fastens his hood with gold, and feasts on a fat swan, all signs of his wealth. Howard confirms that the monk has abandoned his religious role when he says, "The monk's furs and gold pin with its 'love knot' show he is an aristocrat, a lusty one who we are told 'loved venerie [sex]'."[32]

The Friar

Chaucer's friar, named Hubert, is a begging friar—that is, he derives his income from begging in the district allotted to him. Though friars are supposed to devote their time to helping the poor, Hubert, who prefers high-class company and visiting the taverns, knows every innkeeper and barmaid better than he knows the needy. He is an expert beggar; he can persuade even the poorest widow to give him a coin. For additional income, he arranges marriages for a fee and hears confessions in return for a gift. He is something of an enter-

Hubert, the begging friar in The Canterbury Tales, *plays the hurdy-gurdy like this musician.*

tainer in that he sings and plays the hurdy-gurdy (an instrument played by turning a crank). He also seduces young women. He dresses in clothes of worsted wool like those of a doctor. His behavior and attire indicate that he has been corrupted by worldly pleasures.

The Merchant

The merchant is an eminent man of business, a respected importer and banker. Wearing a beaver hat and leather boots, he sits high on his horse. He offers his opinions and explains his activities in quiet, serious tones. However, he has a secret: He is in debt. Although a commoner, the merchant is one of the pilgrims with status.

The Oxford Cleric

The Oxford cleric, or clerk, as he is sometimes called, is the ideal man of learning, someone who has devoted his time to scholarship instead of acquiring wealth. His thin horse, hollow look, and threadbare coat prove that he is devoted to the life of the underpaid scholar. This cleric is happy just to learn and to teach. He prefers books to clothes; he is also unassuming and speaks in the formal tones of an academician, and then only when absolutely necessary. According to Chaucer, good, truly religious clerics are poor, and the bad ones live in luxury. This cleric, therefore, represents virtues that Chaucer held dear.

The Sergeant at the Law

The sergeant at the law is a well-known, respected lawyer who charges large fees for his services. Thanks to his accumulated wealth, he has considerable social status. He wears a variegated coat with a striped silk belt, an indication of his wealth. He knows all the medieval laws and important cases. In a discreet way, he uses this knowledge and his wise sayings to garner respect. He has bought many properties and secured them with perfect titles. Although Chaucer is critical of displays of wealth by pilgrims of the religious orders, he treats the sergeant's accumulation of wealth with sympathy.

The Franklin

Traveling with the sergeant at the law is the franklin, a gentleman of considerable status and wealth, although he ranks below a nobleman. This franklin, with a red face and white beard, is a cheerful man. He lives for the pleasure of food and drink and sets an abundant table of delicate dishes and fine wines to entertain the community and display his wealth. Chaucer says that he keeps partridges in his coops and fish in his pond. Hanging from his belt are a dagger and a small silk purse as white as milk, another sign of wealth in a society in which most people wear well-used purses made of rough, dirty leather.

The Haberdasher, the Dyer, the Carpenter, the Weaver, and the Carpet Maker

These five pilgrims travel together. The haberdasher, who makes men's clothing; the dyer, who dyes cloth; the carpenter; the weaver; and the carpet maker display shiny new tools of their trades. They seem worthy men, successful members of their respective guilds and proud of the way they provide for their wives. They have hired a cook to prepare their food on the trip. None of them tells a story; Chaucer may have intended a story for each but died before completing them.

The Cook

Chaucer describes the kinds of dishes the cook makes. The cook knows well how to flavor food and roast, broil, or fry meat. He makes thick soups and the best milk pudding, and he bakes fine pies. Unfortunately, however, he has an open sore on his knee, suggesting that the cook's hygiene might be less than perfect. Juxtaposing the fact that the cook has a sore beside the praise for his cooking skills is one of Chaucer's many techniques of humor; the surprise combination would have brought a laugh from readers in medieval times.

The Skipper

The skipper, or shipman, has traveled the world in his ship, the *Magdalen,* and knows the seas as well as the rivers in England and Spain. On the pilgrimage he rides a large farm horse, but—as might be expected of one who has spent his life at sea—with little skill. Tanned and weathered, he wears a long woolen gown and has a dagger hanging in a strap around his neck. In the past, while making stops at ports in the wine country, he took advantage of the wine cargo and drank many traders' wines while they slept. He has fought battles, captured prisoners, and without conscience sent them off the plank. But his knowledge of tides, currents, and harbors is without match. Chaucer's description of the skipper is typical of his attitude toward human faults: Chaucer never fails to observe them, but he takes an objective attitude and finds good qualities to balance the faults.

The Doctor of Medicine

The doctor, Chaucer says, uses astrology to guide his practice of healing. To obtain medicines, he makes deals that increase profits both for himself and for apothecaries (pharmacists); yet he is tight with his money. He dresses in bright red and blue garments lined with silk, which are, as Malone points out, "the garb usual for prosperous members of his profession."[33] He eats a nourishing diet good for his digestive system. The doctor reads the works of medical philosophers, but he

Chaucer's doctor relies on astrology in his practice of medicine. Pictured is a diagram of the twelve signs of the zodiac.

seldom reads the Bible. In his description of the doctor, Chaucer mocks the hypocrisy he saw in society: In a supposedly religious age, the doctor has rejected religion for astrology and philosophy and acts to obtain wealth rather than to serve.

The Wife of Bath

Wearing a set of spurs, the wife of Bath, who is an experienced rider, sits easily on her horse. She is pleasingly stout, has gaps between her teeth, and is partially deaf. She is dressed in red stockings, fine leather shoes, a bright kerchief, and a broad-brimmed hat. Her Sunday "kerchiefs were of finely woven ground; /I dared have sworn they weighed a good ten pound."[34] She has traveled widely, having visited Cologne and Rome and made three trips to Jerusalem. She has had five husbands in addition to the lovers she had in her youth. Chaucer blends the wife's positive traits with those less flattering, a blending he uses often.

The Parson

The parson is an educated and saintly man. Like the Oxford cleric, he is poor in material goods, but his mind and soul are rich in thoughts and good works. Rather than running off to London to find an endowment, he stays with his parishioners to teach and preach the gospel to them. He believes in leading by example, regularly visiting the sick and giving from church offerings and his own property to help the poor. Throughout *The Canterbury Tales* Chaucer distinguishes between those who present a facade of holiness and those who are truly holy. The parson, he says, has true holiness, "A holy-minded man of good renoun."[35]

The Plowman

The plowman is the brother of the parson. He is a hard worker, Chaucer implies, saying he is a farmer who has

The plowman, shown in this woodcut, is hardworking and honest.

thrashed his corn (grain), made ditches, and hauled manure
—all mundane farm tasks. Like his brother, he is honest and
pays his tithes (a tenth of his income given to the church)
when they are due. When he helps his neighbor, he tries to
do it without pay. His simple, honest life makes him a peace-
ful man. He wears a tunic and rides a mare.

The Miller

The miller is a big, brawny man with a red beard; a wart with a hair growing from it on his nose; wide, black nostrils; and a wide mouth. A man of little refinement, he brags that he can tear a door off its hinges by running at it like a ram. He wears a white coat and blue hood and has a sword and shield at his side. The miller is dishonest, too. Chaucer says that by placing his thumb on the scale, he charges his customers three times the amount they should pay. He plays the bagpipes and leads the pilgrims out of town as they begin their pilgrimage. The seemingly unrelated facts about the miller illustrate Chaucer's skill at selecting details that together portray an individual. As Malone points out, "The miller's talents as a wrestler, and as an opener of doors, have no direct connection, it is true, with his thumb of gold, but they befit this calling, and his station in life."[36]

The Manciple

In medieval England a manciple was a buyer of provisions. This manciple manages provisions for the Inner Temple, part of the system for training lawyers in England. Chaucer indicates that he is capable of shady dealings, saying that he buys food supplies with such careful planning that he always has money left over from what is given him for that purpose. Though illiterate, he is wiser than his learned masters who have the qualifications to manage estates. The manciple knows the law and can outdo all of his masters, but not always fairly. Howard says, "At the bottom rank among the Canterbury pilgrims is the Manciple, a steward at one of the Inns of Court, very clever at cheating his masters."[37]

The Reeve

A reeve was an official on a manor, someone who interceded between the lord and the serfs. This reeve is ill-tempered and feared by the serfs and herdsmen below him; however, he bargains well for the lord above him and has a nice house as a reward. He keeps accurate records, is a skilled carpenter, and manages the crops and animals well. His master trusts him to care for his sheep, hens, pigs, horses, and cattle and to study the weather conditions in order to calculate the amount of seed needed for a crop and to assess the harvest yield for the season. He has a bowl haircut, no beard, and skinny legs. Riding a gray farm horse named Scot, he wears a long blue overcoat. Howard describes him as "choleric, querulous, old."[38]

The Summoner

A summoner in medieval England was the church official responsible for calling people to appear before an ecclesiastical court to face charges of misdeeds, such as failing to pay church dues or committing adultery. This summoner has a red face covered with large white pimples, black bushy eyebrows, eyes like slits, and a skimpy beard. His breath smells of onions, garlic, and strong red wine. He frightens children. He pursues women for sex and willingly offers his mistress to another man for a quart of wine. When he is drunk, he speaks only Latin—two or three phrases he has memorized but does not understand. He is, however, a kind, gentle rascal, who knows the people's secrets and, for a price, will keep them from the archdeacon. He wears a large garland on his head and engages the friar in a quarrel during "The Wife of Bath's Tale." In his description of the summoner, Chaucer displays his skill at selecting details that portray a crude, revolting, immoral character, yet he adds, as he usually does when noting faults, a kind word, perhaps with tongue in cheek.

The Pardoner

In medieval times a pardoner had authority from the pope to sell indulgences—to provide forgiveness for sins or to extend the time before a guilty person had to atone for his or her sin before being punished. This pardoner, riding with his friend

Church officials sell indulgences. Almost every church official in
The Canterbury Tales *is corrupt in some way.*

the summoner, is just back from Rome with a bagful of fake
relics (small objects serving as tokens of early Christianity)
that he sells at high prices to good country parsons and their
parishioners. He has thin yellow hair hanging over his shoul-
ders, eyes that bug out, no beard, and a goatlike voice. He
sings, and the summoner harmonizes with a beautiful trumpet

49

sound. The pardoner is a noble churchman, and on Sunday he reads the lesson effectively, sings the offertory, and preaches with a silver tongue. Compared with the summoner, as Michael Hoy points out, "there is something more subtly repulsive about the Pardoner. His appearance is effeminate, with long fair hair and staring eyes. . . . His soft, high-pitched, bleating voice and his smooth complexion emphasize this."[39]

The Host
The host of the Tabard Inn, Harry Bailly, welcomes the company of pilgrims and serves them good food and wine. He is the one who suggests the contest of telling stories and promises a free supper for the teller of the best tale. He also agrees to guide the group.

CHAPTER FOUR

The Plots

Each story within *The Canterbury Tales* has its own discrete plot. What links these individual tales is the pilgrimage in which each person telling a tale is supposedly engaged. This literary device by which individual tales are loosely connected is called a frame story. Within this frame, Chaucer collects a variety of stories, among them the four major types of stories common at the time: romance, beast fable, fabliau, and exemplum.

A *romance* is a story involving knights, kings, or high-born men and women who act in search of love, salvation, or adventure.

A *beast fable* is a story in which the characters are animals that talk; the animals are often imbued with human qualities and are used to put forth a satiric comment on the church or the lives of the nobility.

A *fabliau* is a humorous, often bawdy, story meant to be read aloud, to appeal to an uneducated audience, and to satirize some aspect of human behavior.

An *exemplum* is a story meant to impart a specific moral point, often using exaggerated or artificial characters or plots.

Since Chaucer died before he finished *The Canterbury Tales,* nobody knows for certain in what order he intended

The town of Canterbury is the destination of Chaucer's pilgrims. Pictured is Canterbury cathedral.

for them to be read. Nineteenth-century scholars placed the tales in groups and the groups in an order that creates a consistent and continuous narrative of a pilgrimage.

Group A
"The Prologue"

The Canterbury Tales opens with "The Prologue," which composes the frame surrounding the tales themselves. "The Prologue" relates how the pilgrims gather at the Tabard Inn on the outskirts of London, from which they will depart on horseback on their pilgrimage to Canterbury, fifty-nine miles away. Chaucer describes the appearance and personality of most of the pilgrims. After the host of the inn, Harry Bailly, serves a meal to the pilgrims, he suggests that they have a contest on the way to see which pilgrim can tell the best story. He offers to lead the group and judge their stories.

"The Knight's Tale"

"The Knight's Tale" is a romance that draws on Greek mythology for its content. In his story, the knight tells how the king of Athens, Theseus, returning to Athens with his new wife, Hippolyta, and her younger sister, Emily, captures two Theban princes, Arcite and Palamon, and imprisons them. The knight then recounts the jealousy between the princes, both of whom fall in love with Emily as she strolls outside their prison window. Arcite is sent back to Thebes, where he languishes because he cannot see Emily. On a tip from Mercury, the messenger god, he returns to Athens disguised as a laborer. Meanwhile, after pining for Emily for seven years, Palamon escapes from prison and hides in a grove, where Arcite coincidentally finds him. They fight for the hand of Emily, but Theseus intervenes and sets up a tournament between the two, to take place later. In the tournament, Arcite is mortally wounded; as he dies, he makes a long speech to Emily, in which he proclaims his love for her. Palamon marries Emily and they live happily thereafter.

"The Miller's Tale"

"The Miller's Tale" is a fabliau in which an Oxford student, Nicholas, outwits a jealous old carpenter, John, in order to have an affair with the carpenter's young wife, Alison. Nicholas persuades John that a flood is coming and that to save themselves the three of them must sleep in tubs suspended from the rafters. At nightfall John, Nicholas, and Alison climb into their tubs. When John falls asleep, Nicholas and Alison climb down and spend the night in bed together. They are enjoying each other when a young cleric named Absolon, also in love with Alison, appears at the window and calls to her. Nicholas thrusts his backside out the window. In the dark, Absolon mistakes Nicholas's rear for Alison's face and tries to kiss it, at which point Nicholas breaks wind. In retaliation, Absolon returns with a hot poker; when Nicholas tries the same trick again, Absolon brands him on the backside. Nicholas screams for water to douse the burn. John, hearing Nicholas screaming about water, thinks the flood has arrived. He cuts the rope holding up his tub and crashes to the floor. A crowd gathers, and John is declared crazy as people laugh at his humiliation at having been so thoroughly hoodwinked.

"The Reeve's Tale"

"The Reeve's Tale" is also a fabliau and is a response to "The Miller's Tale." In this tale, two students, Alan and John, get the best of a dishonest miller named Simpkin the Swagger. The students are determined not to be cheated, but Simpkin lets loose their horse, and while they chase it all around the countryside, the miller steals part of their grain. It is evening by the time the two return with their horse, so they ask to stay the night in the miller's one-room house. During the night, Alan seduces the miller's daughter, and John seduces the miller's wife. The miller finds out, and a fight ensues in the pitch-dark room. Alan and John recover their grain and leave the miller humiliated and unpaid for grinding their grain.

"The Cook's Tale"

"The Cook's Tale" is one of two tales Chaucer left unfinished. Chaucer begins a story about Reveller Peterkin, an apprentice who skips work to dance, sing, and play dice. When Peterkin steals from his master's till, the master fires him, and the tale stops there.

Group B

"The Man of Law's Tale"

"The Man of Law's Tale" is a romance about the misfortunes that beautiful Constance undergoes as the obedient daughter of a Christian Roman emperor. She is first sent to Syria to be the wife of the Muslim sultan, who promises to convert to Christianity in order to marry Constance. The sultan's mother, however, objects to her son's marriage; there is a fight among Christians and Muslims, during which the sultan is killed; and the mother sends Constance back to Rome. The boat goes off course and ends up in Northumberland. There, Constance meets and marries the pagan king Alla. She bears him a child, Maurice, but Alla's cruel mother uses trickery to have Constance once again set adrift at sea, along with Maurice. She and her son eventually get safely back to Rome. Alla later finds them and brings them back to Northumberland. Alla dies a year after recovering

Chaucer's man of law tells of the tribulations of the beautiful and pious Constance.

his wife and child, and Constance and Maurice return to Rome and live in the home of the emperor until Constance later dies. Chaucer does not tell what happens to Maurice.

"The Shipman's Tale"

"The Shipman's Tale" is a fabliau about a naive, money-loving merchant, his beautiful wife, and their friend, a monk named Sir John. While the merchant is occupied counting his money, the wife and the monk walk in the garden, where she tells the monk that she is dissatisfied with her husband's sexual performance. She also asks for a loan of a hundred francs to buy clothes. The two embrace and agree to a sexual encounter while the merchant is out of town. The monk borrows the hundred francs from the merchant and then gives it to the wife following their brief affair. When the merchant returns, the monk tells him that he has repaid the loan by giving the money to his wife. The merchant admonishes his wife for not telling him she had gotten the money from Sir John, never suspecting that she had been unfaithful. The wife is outraged but lets on that it is because Sir John led her to believe the money was for her to use for clothes. The story ends with the merchant none the wiser, telling his wife to be more moderate in her spending.

"The Prioress's Tale"

"The Prioress's Tale" is a miracle story that Chaucer may have intended as a critique of anti-Semitic attitudes. It tells of a seven-year-old Christian boy who sings the praises of Mary, mother of Jesus, as he walks through the Jewish section of town as he goes to and from school. The prioress says the Jews, offended by the boy's song, hire a murderer who slits the boy's throat and throws his body into a privy. When the boy fails to come home, his mother searches for him. God, the prioress says, has miraculously given the boy power to sing by placing a seed on his tongue, and the mother hears the singing. The body is recovered and taken to the abbey, and those who arranged for his murder are caught and violently punished. The abbot removes the seed, after which the boy stops singing and is buried in a marble tomb. Chaucer meant for his readers to note the prioress's virulent anti-Semitism but also to see her extreme views as absurd.

"The Tale of Sir Topaz"

When the host asks Chaucer himself to tell his tale, Chaucer pleads that he is a dunce, but the host persists. Chaucer relents, and the tale he tells of the knight Sir Topaz is a parody of a romance and a satire on knighthood. Sir Topaz, who has fallen in love with an elf queen, rides out into the fairy country, where he encounters a three-headed giant named Sir Olifaunt. He rushes home for his armor, which he puts on with elaborate ritual. He returns to fairy country to meet the giant; on the way he sleeps in the open and drinks only pure spring water. The reader never learns what happens because the host interrupts Chaucer, chiding him for telling such a "dull" tale. Chaucer deliberately tells the tale in bad rhyme and rhythm and uses tiresome clichés to heighten the absurdity of the hero and his adventures.

Chaucer's "Tale of Melibeus"

Having been chided for his "Tale of Sir Topaz," Chaucer then tells "The Tale of Melibeus," which debates whether violence should be avenged with violence or forgiven. Melibeus's daughter Sophia has been assaulted and wounded by three enemies. Melibeus wants revenge, but he calls a council to advise him. The council of young and old bring up conflicting arguments and opinions, and the discussion turns into a shouting match. The council members take a vote, but Melibeus disagrees with the decision, which, he believes, is too lenient. The conflict between Melibeus and the council reaches a stalemate. In the end, Sophia's mother, Dame

The Canterbury pilgrims tell a variety of stories during their journey, each with a unique plot.

Prudence, prevails on her husband to conclude that forgiveness is the best response.

"The Monk's Tale"

"The Monk's Tale" does not fit the model of any of the four major types of stories but instead illustrates how Chaucer defined tragedy. The monk tells the stories of seventeen individuals—some mythical, some historical—who achieve high places and are brought down by Fortune. They range from Satan to Hercules and Samson, from Julius Caesar to King Peter of Spain. In some cases the narrator suggests a specific moral failing that leads to the individual's fall, but other times it seems ill fortune visits even those who deserve otherwise. Some of the figures, such as the biblical king Nebuchadnezzar, the Roman emperor Nero, and the Greek king Croesus, suffer in addition to being brought low because they were cruel or excessively proud. Others, such as Samson, King Peter of Spain, and Count Ugolino of Pisa, suffer because they were the victims of someone else's deception. Most of the individuals die in the end.

"The Nun's Priest's Tale"

"The Nun's Priest's Tale" is something of a hybrid, being primarily a beast fable but containing elements of romance and exemplum. A rooster and seven hens live on the farm of a poor widow and her two daughters. On their perch, the rooster Chanticleer and his wife Pertelope discuss at length the meaning of Chanticleer's dream in which he is captured by a fox. Pertelope and Chanticleer get into a quarrel over the proper way to respond to the dream. Pertelope takes a pragmatic approach and tells her husband to take medicine found in the barnyard plants; Chanticleer reviews various theories about the importance of dreams. Later, on the ground, Chanticleer meets the fox. Chanticleer is at first on his guard, but the fox flatters him into crowing with his eyes closed. This gives the fox a chance to grab the rooster by his neck. The hens, the widow, her daughters, and all of the other farm animals noisily pursue the fox. Chanticleer has the presence of mind to tell the fox to yell at his pursuers to turn back. When the fox opens his mouth to talk, Chanticleer gets loose and flies into a tree. In a final exchange, both fox and rooster admit their mistakes, and the narrator warns the reader to beware of flatterers.

Group C

"The Physician's Tale"

"The Physician's Tale" is a shocking story, the main idea of which is abuse of power and justice. In the tale a beautiful, virtuous girl, Virginia, is the object of a lecherous judge's desire. The judge, Appius, hatches a plot to take Virginia from her parents, enslave her, and rape her. Helpless against the judge's power, Virginius, the girl's father, can choose between allowing his daughter to be dishonored or killing her to keep her from Appius's clutches. He therefore beheads Virginia and places her head on the judge's bench. The community rises up, exiles the accomplice who helped the judge with his plot, and imprisons the judge, who then hangs himself. The story is indeed about Virginia's virtues and suffering, but, as Velma Bourgeois Richmond says, "The tale, then, has much to say about justice, or rather its lack in a corrupt official like Appius."[40]

"The Pardoner's Tale"

For his tale, the pardoner delivers one of the sermons he preaches from the pulpit. He begins by railing against the sins of gluttony, drunkenness, swearing, and gambling. Then he presents his exemplum, a story about three drunken youths who vow to find and kill Death. They meet an old man who says he hopes to die. When asked where Death might be, the old man points the three to an oak tree, where they find eight bushels of gold coins. One youth goes to town for food and drink and plots to have all the gold for himself by poisoning the other two. The two left guarding the gold plan to stab the one who goes to town in order to divide the gold between them. Both plans work: The two conspirators take the poisoned provisions, but before the deadly poison has started to work, they kill the man who has poisoned them. As a result, all three die. The pardoner finishes his sermon by offering his power of pardon to anyone willing to pay and unabashedly asks for money. Trevor Whittock, in *A Reading of the "Canterbury Tales,"* offers this opinion:

> *The Pardoner's Tale* demonstrates, in a way that is both more startling and more true, the rewards of sin. The

Pardoner is a complete scoundrel, perhaps the most vicious of all the pilgrims, and proud of it. In the *Prologue* he boasts of his vices, and in his tale displays the cunning of his tongue. . . . His hypocrisy masks a boundless contempt for those he dupes, and he exults in his own motives.[41]

Group D

"The Wife of Bath's Tale"

"The Wife of Bath's Tale" is preceded by a prologue of its own—one that is longer than the tale itself. In the prologue, she tells how she managed to get the upper hand with each of her five husbands. The wife of Bath then commences her tale, which is a romance about a knight who rapes a maiden. The queen, who takes charge of his punishment, gives him a year in which to discover what women most desire. At the end of his time, an old lady tells him that a woman most wants sovereignty over her husband. The old woman, who is really the queen in disguise, tricks the knight into marrying her; he resists but cannot avoid the marriage. The woman argues the virtues of an older wife. The knight is asked to decide which is better: a wife that is ugly

The wife of Bath boasts how she has dominated each of her five husbands.

and faithful or one that is beautiful and unfaithful. When he forfeits his opportunity to choose, she doffs her disguise and the knight finds himself married to a beautiful young woman, with whom he lives happily. Whittock concludes, "The knight chooses rightly by giving the choice to her. . . . Thus, in the mutual recognition of the other, in each giving only to find that the giving is the taking, in this lies the ideal love-marriage relationship. This is the true moral of the *Tale*."[42]

"The Friar's Tale"

"The Friar's Tale" satirizes a summoner who earns his money dishonestly by making false charges and taking bribes. In the tale, the summoner forms a pact with a yeoman, who is the devil in disguise. In their pact, they agree to stay together and support each other. They see a farmer urging his horses to pull his cart from the mud; in frustration, the farmer wishes his horses and cart to the devil. The summoner urges the fiend to take them, but the fiend recognizes that the farmer's oath is not his true intent. They then go to the home of a poor widow; here, the summoner demands twelve pence, which she does not have. He says if she does not pay, the devil will fetch him, and she says to let him. Because the widow meant

In the friar's tale, a summoner ends up in hell after trying to take money from a poor widow.

what she said, the devil whisks the summoner off to a special place in hell reserved for summoners. The central idea of this tale is knowing if what is said is what is intended.

"The Summoner's Tale"

"The Summoner's Tale" is preceded by a prologue in which the summoner tells of an angel who takes a friar to hell to see where friars dwell. Satan has a broad tail, and when it is lifted, twenty thousand friars swarm out from Satan's "arse," fly around, and then return. The summoner goes on to tell his tale, in which a friar visits the home of Thomas and pressures him to contribute to the church. Each time the friar begs, the language and pressure increase, as if the bigger the lie the more effective it is. Finally, Thomas agrees to give what he has and invites the friar to search behind his back to find his contribution. At the appropriate moment, Thomas emits a gigantic, loud fart. The insulted friar goes to the lord of the manor and rages about the trick played on him, and the lord listens and believes him. The incident mocks King Richard, who, Chaucer thought, coddled corrupt friars, a group that Chaucer disliked. The crudeness of the tale guaranteed that readers would see its satirical intent.

Group E
"The Clerk's Tale"

"The Clerk's Tale" tells of Walter, a wealthy marquis, and his marriage to the good and beautiful peasant girl Griselda, who promises always to obey her husband's wishes. After a few happy years, Walter plans ways to test Griselda's loyalty; he takes away their daughter and four years later does the same with their son; he divorces her, takes a young, beautiful bride, and asks Griselda to return to the castle to decorate for the wedding. With every test, Griselda graciously accommodates her husband's wishes. Finally, Walter admits that he was testing

Griselda and takes her in his arms. The divorce was fake, and the young woman he pretended to want to marry is in reality their daughter, whom Walter had hidden in Bologna with his sister and now has returned along with their son. Griselda is restored as his wife, and the united family lives happily. The clerk directly contradicts the wife of Bath by telling a tale about a marriage in which the wife is completely dominated by her husband. Bernard F. Huppe says, "In the face of his [Walter's] sadistic wilfullness Griselda's patience appears masochistic; in any real world her behavior as an ideal of wifely conduct is intolerable, more unacceptable even than the Wife's ideal of wifely despotism."[43]

"The Merchant's Tale"

"The Merchant's Tale" is about January, an Italian knight who has been a bachelor all his life and who, at age sixty, wants to take a wife. He finds a beautiful young woman named May, whom he urges his friends to procure for him. They do this, but at the wedding feast the knight's squire, Damian, falls in love with May, and secretly they exchange notes. January is happy in his marriage to May until suddenly he loses his sight. Now, Damian and May plot to meet near a pear tree in the garden when May walks there with January. Damian hides in the pear tree, and May tricks January into helping her climb the tree to get a pear. While Damian and May embrace in the pear tree, January magically regains his sight. When he sees what is happening, he accuses May of being unfaithful. May insists that the old man's newly regained sight is unreliable and that she is innocent, and January believes her. With this story, Chaucer illustrates a kind of marriage in which the mismatched participants have neither loyalty nor love. In *Of Sondry Folk: The Dramatic Principle in the "Canterbury Tales,"* R.M. Lumiansky says, "There is nothing at all appealing or cheerful about the Merchant's story. In its cold intellectualism, its lack of genial raillery or healthy animal enjoyment, and

The blind old knight of "The Merchant's Tale" miraculously regains his sight only to witness the infidelity of his young wife.

in its piling up of sharply satiric details, it conveys a bitter irony unique in Chaucer's writings."[44]

Group F

"The Squire's Tale"

One of the two unfinished tales (the other is "The Cook's Tale"), "The Squire's Tale" begins a story of King Camuskan, his wife, two sons, and daughter, Canace. During the king's birthday feast, a knight rides in on a brass steed carrying gifts of a mirror, a ring, and a sword. All have magical properties: The brass horse provides a ride through the air when the rider operates the pins in its ears, the mirror foretells the truth, the ring interprets the language of birds, and the sword both cuts and heals. With the ring in hand, Canace hears the sad story of a female falcon whose lover has left her for another bird. Canace makes a home for the falcon and nurses it. The squire promises to tell of the king's adventures and of the happy resolution to the falcon's troubles. The story stops there, however; Chaucer may have intended to provide further stories involving the brass horse and the other magical gifts, but scholars have no proof of this.

"The Franklin's Tale"

"The Franklin's Tale" is a romance. When the knight Arveragus marries Lady Dorigen, he promises to obey her, and she promises to be humble and loyal. While Arveragus is away on a knightly venture, his squire, Aurelius, asks for Dorigen's love; she chooses to remain loyal to her husband, but to soften her rejection, she tells Aurelius that he can be her lover only when he has cleared the jagged rocks from the coastline and made it safe for ships. Aurelius hires a magician to raise the water level enough to make the rocks invisible and expects Dorigen to keep her word. Arveragus, who has come home, urges his wife to honor her word with Aurelius. Dorigen cries at the prospect of taking Aurelius as her lover, and when Aurelius sees the tearful Dorigen, he releases her of her pledge. The magician, hearing of Aurelius's honor, cancels the charges for his service. In this tale, Chaucer reflects on the ideals of marriage and knighthood, but he recognizes the difficulty of fulfilling the ideals of both. As Richmond says, "Seeing, perception, is a crucial theme in the *Franklin's Tale,* which begins with a clear affirmation of love, gentilesse, truth, and so on. The values are easy to define, but seeing how to embody them is another matter, for there are many appearances that prove false."[45]

Group G
"The Second Nun's Tale"

"The Second Nun's Tale" recounts the life of St. Cecilia, who has a guardian angel. When Cecilia marries Valerian, she persuades him of the value of chastity and of a heavenly afterlife and converts him to Christianity. St. Urban baptizes him, and Valerian sees the angel. Cecilia and Valerian then convert Valerian's brother, Tiburce. For refusing to sacrifice to Jove, Roman officers behead Valerian and Tiburce and burn Cecilia. Her house becomes the Church of Saint Cecilia. In *Chaucer's Drama of Style: Poetic Variety and Contrast in the "Canterbury Tales,"* C. David Benson says, *"The Second Nun's Tale* is fundamentally a poem about conversion, not just the exterior conversion from pagan to Christian (though this is important), but the deeper conversion from earthly to spiritual values."[46]

"The Canon's Yeoman's Tale"

A canon (a secular priest) and his yeoman ride up in haste to catch the pilgrims, who are already well on their way. The canon leaves, misunderstanding something the yeoman said, and never returns to tell a tale. The yeoman explains how, for seven years, he has tried to learn alchemy from the canon, but all of his efforts have failed. He then tells about a priest who was fooled by another canon, who used tricks to teach the priest how to turn mercury and copper into silver. After paying the canon fees, the priest tried to replicate the procedures, but, of course, they failed. At first the priest seems to deserve sympathy, but, on second thought, he does not because he has turned his attention from priestly duties. According to Whittock, "The theme of the *Prologue* and *Tale* is the misuse of

The canon's yeoman tells of a priest who strays from his religious duties in order to learn alchemy.

men's intelligence in the obsessive pursuit of false and meretricious [pretentious] goals."[47]

Group H

"The Manciple's Tale"

"The Manciple's Tale" contains elements of magic. In this tale, Phoebus (Apollo) is a handsome man, an excellent marksman, and a skilled musician who loves his wife and diligently tries to please her, but he is a jealous husband. In a cage he keeps a white crow with a beautiful voice trained to mimic the tone and words of any man. When Phoebus is away, his wife sends for her lover, a low-class man with a poor reputation. Phoebus returns, and the crow tells him a man has slept with his wife. In a jealous rage, Phoebus kills his wife, breaks all of his musical instruments, and pulls out the crow's white feathers, makes it black, and replaces its beautiful voice with a croaking noise. Then Phoebus regrets his actions and wishes he were dead. The manciple gives his story the quality of an exemplum by providing two morals: not to strike too soon and not to tell bad news. Richmond says, "Restraint in speech is urged; more specifically 'A wikked tonge is worse than a feend.'. . . Given the proclivities of the pilgrims to quarrel and be personally and professionally abusive, this is indeed a pointed satiric warning. Explicitly, God finds 'janglers' (chatterers) abominable."[48]

Group I
"The Parson's Tale"

The parson does not tell a story but tells instead a prose tale, or sermon, explaining the necessary readiness for confession and the meaning of the seven deadly sins. Preparation for confession requires penitence—regretting sin and having the will to refrain from it—and an attitude of contrition and sorrow. Pride, or arrogance, is one of the deadly sins, and it can be remedied by humility. Envy and sorrow for the good fortunes of others can be remedied with love for God and neighbors. Spontaneous and premeditated anger can be remedied with patience. One who slacks in his or her tasks is guilty of sloth and can, with fortitude, remedy the fault. Avarice is the excessive desire for worldly things and can be remedied by pity, according to the parson. Gluttony and drunkenness require abstinence and temperance to be remedied. Lechery is stealing another's body and soul; its remedy is chastity. A sinner must confess his sins honestly and, in order to gain satisfaction, give penance. Huppe says:

> The *Canterbury Tales* ends on a note of solemn, high seriousness, with the *Parson's Tale* and *Chaucer's Retractions,* but this highly serious vision of man's difficult

pilgrimage through the world provides the effective symbol for all the narratives which have preceded it. . . . Further, the perception of the moral design of the *Canterbury Tales* gives the poem its full amplitude as high comedy, embodying a vision of life which sees the shadows of human weakness and the brightness of human aspiration.[49]

CHAPTER FIVE

Literary Devices and Themes

More than six hundred years after the work was created, *The Canterbury Tales* is outstanding for the modernity of its themes and of the literary devices Chaucer employed. Many of the tales are rewritten from earlier works by other writers, but in weaving them together within the frame of the account of a pilgrimage, Chaucer imbued those works with new meaning, highlighting themes that were timely and, as history has proven, timeless.

The Pilgrimage as a Metaphor

Using a pilgrimage to unify a collection of stories was a new idea when Chaucer wrote *The Canterbury Tales*. The pilgrimage as a literary device works on a variety of levels. At first glance, "The Prologue," which first sets out for readers the circumstances of the pilgrimage, appears to be a literal account of a particular medieval pilgrimage. Chaucer identifies the time of year, April, and the location of the starting point, the Tabard Inn. He identifies the pilgrims as they gather for the evening meal and gives the time their journey will start, dawn, names the towns they will pass through, and gives the expected ending time, sunset.

He describes the journey as both a religious and a social event during which the pilgrims listen to each other and banter back and forth in the links between stories. Such a pilgrimage would have been familiar to a medieval audience; journeys of this sort were undertaken, usually in the spring, for some material, moral, or spiritual benefit. In his article "The Social and Literary Scene in England," Paul Strohm sums up the pilgrimage by saying, "The pilgrimage itself is, after all, a social as well as a religious event, with individuals interacting according to their social perspectives as expressed by their class (or rank) and vocation."[50]

A closer look at "The Prologue," however, suggests that Chaucer intended for readers to interpret the pilgrimage less literally. First, Chaucer's pilgrims make the trip to Canterbury too quickly. Chaucer's contemporaries would have known that, on horseback, this trip of fifty-nine miles in reality would have taken travelers three or four days. Second, Chaucer depicts thirty people riding horses and listening to one pilgrim telling a story. In *Chapters on Chaucer*, Kemp Malone suggests how impractical a storytelling contest on horseback would have been.

> Picture in your mind's eye thirty-odd pilgrims on horseback, strung out for a quarter of a mile on the Canterbury road, trying to listen to one of their number who is telling a tale as they ride along. How well could they hear him? Those nearest to the teller of the tale might hear much of it, though even they would miss a good deal. The rest of the pilgrims (by far the greatest number) would hear nothing, or, at most, would hear the speaker's voice without being able to make out the words.[51]

Just as those reading in Chaucer's era would have known the impossibility of traveling from London to Canterbury in a day, so too would they have recognized the flaw inherent in conducting a story contest on horseback. Clearly, Chaucer meant for the pilgrimage to be seen differently, as a metaphor.

When *The Canterbury Tales* is taken as a whole, the pilgrimage can be seen as a metaphor for the human journey of life in general. In his essay "Chaucerian Realism," Morton W. Bloomfield explains that comparing life to a religious pilgrimage would likely have made sense to Chaucer's readers:

> The pilgrimage is also the key metaphor for life from the religious sphere. We are all pilgrims on the way to the heavenly city, and every journey, but especially the religious one, reflects the basic pattern of existence. We are all homeless, exiled from paradise, looking for a return to our home which is heaven, of which the earthly paradise was the foreshadowing. No doubt Chaucer had this religious dimension in mind when he chose a pilgrimage as a frame.[52]

For their part, the pilgrims and their stories are metaphors for the human condition. Chaucer portrays typical religious and working people from medieval England. They are varied in their morality, desires, and emotions, as literary scholar Ralph Baldwin describes:

> The waywardness and frailty of the characters, the too human gropings and anguish, the tears and tumult, diversions and banter, the self-indulgences and the heroism, tensions, and tenderness, the hypocrisies and rue; these are the actions of that feckless [flawed] creature man in his human comedy.[53]

When this diverse gathering of humans comes to the end of its journey at sunset near Canterbury, the parson speaks last. In the parson's prologue, Chaucer makes clear his intent that this pilgrimage be seen symbolically, presaging a spiritual journey:

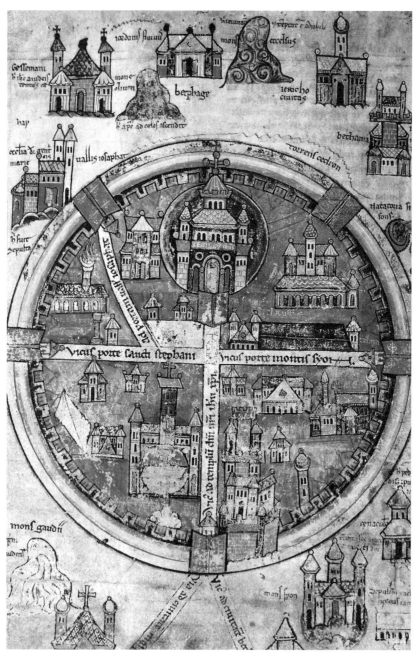

This medieval map shows Jerusalem, one of the holiest destinations for pilgrims. The Canterbury pilgrimage may be interpreted as a metaphor for the spiritual pilgrimage to Jerusalem.

A happy thing, to knit and make an end
Of all our feast. Jesu in mercy send
Me wit to guide your way one further stage
Upon that perfect, glorious pilgrimage
Called the celestial, to Jerusalem.[54]

The Role of the Host

Beyond functioning as a metaphor, the pilgrimage serves to unify what would otherwise seem a rather random selection of stories. In his role of judge of the stories and unofficial leader, the host also plays a vital role in creating unity in *The Canterbury Tales*. The host has an obvious presence in the prologue and in the links between stories, keeping the storytelling moving.

Harry Bailly was in fact a real person, but the Harry Bailly portrayed in the *The Canterbury Tales* is not designed to be taken seriously in the literal sense. For example, he is the opposite of a gracious innkeeper. Chaucer says that he is fit to be a marshal. According to Malone, "Chaucer's account is humorous from start to finish, the host telling the pilgrims what to do and the pilgrims obeying his orders in comic reversal of the customary relationship between an innkeeper and his guests. The host begins by using a little flattery before bringing forward his proposal."[55] Ironically, the host repeatedly asserts in the links between the tales that he is a henpecked husband.

The host's most important role in terms of plot is to organize the storytelling and keep the stories coming. He begins by having pilgrims draw the shortest straw to be the first teller. After the knight wins the right to tell the first story, the host simply calls on pilgrims without warning. Only once does a pilgrim dispute the host's request: When the host calls on the monk, the miller demands to be next. The host gives in and comments, "Well, blast you then, you may."[56] Usually the pilgrims comply, as the prioress does when the host says, "I'd

The Canterbury pilgrims enjoy a meal at the Tabard Inn before setting out on their journey. Their host, innkeeper Harry Bailly, organizes and judges the storytelling contest.

judge it time for you to show your skill/By telling the next story, if you will./Will you vouchsafe, dear lady, to comply?"[57]

Besides organizing the story contest, the host settles disputes. When the reeve complains that the miller's story insults him, the host speaks "as lordly as a king," ignores the reeve's protest, and simply tells him, "High time to tell your story, so begin it."[58] Later, when the friar interrupts the wife of Bath's story, a squabble erupts between him and the summoner. The host calls to them, "Be quiet, that's enough!/Shut up, and let the woman tell her tale."[59] The host continues to speak in the same blunt, authoritarian manner.

The host is as free with his opinions of stories as he is with his orders to pilgrims. After the shipman has told his tale, the host tells him he has spoken well and wishes him a long life. When the knight interrupts the monk's long collection of tragedies, the host tells the monk that he talks too loud and his stories are boring. "Such talk as that's not worth a butter-fly."[60] He praises the nun's priest for a merry tale of Chanticleer and the squire for speaking like a gentleman. To the physician's tale about the father who beheaded his daughter to avoid being dishonored by a judge, the host speaks many lines about the poor beautiful girl and calls for death to all cheating and despicable judges. The host's assumption that his opinions are important and that people want to hear them is in keeping with his original assumption that people want to take his orders.

In short, the host's status as an outsider among the pilgrims belies the significance of his constant presence. He is not, however, the only outsider on the journey.

Chaucer's Voices

Chaucer goes along with the pilgrims on the trip to Canterbury and reports the stories they tell, but like the host, he is outside the pilgrim community. Still, Chaucer has his own opinions, which he sometimes states directly but more often conveys through the voices of a character in a tale or one of the pilgrims.

When Chaucer speaks directly to the reader, it is with the intent of providing specific guidance. Before every tale he tells what is happening on the pilgrimage and in the story-telling contest. For example, he tells when the wife of Bath ends her prologue and when the host compliments the ship-man and turns to the prioress.

At the end of the account of the journey, Chaucer speaks in his own voice one last time, asking God to remember those tales that lead to virtue and to forgive him for those he tells about human vanity. Here Chaucer speaks in the mode of a teacher and a spiritual person. Bloomfield says, "The creator

of these titles and comments is not the pilgrim who is report-
ing the Canterbury pilgrimage, although he is related to him
closely. He is speaking to us from another part of his being."[61]

Most of the time Chaucer speaks like an actor taking on
different roles. One role is the disclaimer, the periodic voice

*Chaucer expresses his own opinions by speaking through the voices of his
pilgrims or through the characters in their tales.*

ironically disavowing responsibility for what is being written. In "The Prologue," for example, Chaucer begs of the reader not to condemn him for using rude language because if he does not record the words as told, his account of the tale would not be true. Furthermore, Chaucer does not want opinions he does not hold attributed to him. In "The Nun's Priest's Tale," when the words of the tale blame and insult women, Chaucer interrupts, "These are the cock's words, and not mine, I'm giving;/I think no harm of any woman living."[62] The recurrence of disclaimers throughout the book contributes unity to the narrative, reminding readers that Chaucer intended for his work to be considered as a whole.

Another role that Chaucer adopts is that of the learned scholar. Throughout the book, this voice interrupts the tales and adds various kinds of background information to illustrate points in the stories. He tells about Adam, Abraham, and Jacob from the Bible, about the Greek myths of Achilles and Pyramus and Thisbe. He quotes from the Greek philosopher Theophrastus and provides information on dream theory and the practice of alchemy. The reader hardly notices these intrusions by the narrator because they are skillfully woven into the pilgrims' tales. Only when one pauses, remembering that few people owned books as Chaucer did, is it apparent that the narrator, not the pilgrim telling the tale, is speaking.

As narrator, Chaucer avoids standing in judgment of his characters. Some of the pilgrims are admirable characters who tell moral tales, but others are crooks, cheats, and wrongdoers, and their tales reflect their failings. Yet throughout *The Canterbury Tales,* Chaucer retains an evenhanded and charitable attitude toward his characters. Baldwin says, "Uniformly with Chaucer there are affection, good will, and objectivity visited upon his characters, so that they get the chance to be what, independently, they *have* to be, given the working out of those characteristics with which they have been endowed."[63]

The fragmentary nature of *The Canterbury Tales* and Chaucer's use of different voices make it challenging to discern a consistent message in every tale. What Chaucer the man values and thinks is hinted at when one looks for recurring themes in the work.

Love and Marriage

Possibly the most obvious theme in *The Canterbury Tales* is the theme of love and marriage and the relationship between husbands and wives. More specifically, Chaucer questions the idea that gender should be the basis for allocating either power or wealth. Such a stance sets Chaucer apart from his contemporaries. During the Middle Ages, wives were expected to be subservient to their husbands, and most women had no way of earning a living. In his essay "The *Canterbury Tales* III: Pathos," Robert Worth Frank Jr. explains:

> We must remember, finally, that obedience was demanded not only by religion but by many social relationships in the fourteenth and fifteenth centuries: wife to husband, fief to feudal lord, subject to superior. Humility and subservience on one side, arrogance and outrageous demand on the other were the order of the day in a society so hierarchical. The strain on psyche and ego may be imagined. And these were the centuries in which that hierarchy was beginning to show signs of stress and change.[64]

The tales as told by Chaucer's characters illustrate a broad range of the ways men and women might interact. Sometimes, Chaucer presents two tales depicting relationships that are mirror images of one another. Other tales depict more subtle variations of traditional gender roles.

The wife of Bath presents a view of marriage and a wife's role most at odds with what most people in medieval society believed. For example, the wife of Bath takes the position

The wife of Bath and the clerk express opposing views on marriage, one of the dominant themes of The Canterbury Tales. *Here, a medieval noble couple is getting married.*

that wives should dominate their husbands. In her prologue, she tells the pilgrims how she has succeeded in making five husbands subservient to her. She also defies the church's promotion of chastity, arguing instead that virginity is overrated and that God provided bodies to be used for sex. Saints, she says, may follow the ideal of chastity if they wish, but it is not her ideal. Moreover, she defies the church's doctrine that a widow or a widower must never remarry. She wonders aloud where in the Bible it says that remarriage is forbidden. In her tale, the wife of Bath clearly states that what women want most in life is sovereignty over their husbands. The wife of

Bath's frank expression of her opinions ignites lively debate among the pilgrims, and the tales that follow frequently touch on the proper relationship between men and women.

To modern readers, the wife of Bath seems particularly likeable. Derek Brewer offers his reaction to the wife's tale: "It is not only because of her modern feelings for the rights of women that we sympathize with her; it is because of her human enjoyment and gusto, her frank acceptance of life and love and of herself."[65]

Yet Chaucer recognized that not everyone in his day could accept the wife of Bath's premise, as "The Clerk's Tale" suggests. In "The Clerk's Tale," a wife is totally subservient to her husband. Griselda remains loyal to her husband even though he puts her through a series of cruel tests. Chaucer himself does not remain completely neutral in this debate. The very improbability of the plot in this tale suggests that Chaucer does not expect the reader to regard this marriage as ideal. Frank comments:

> For some [readers], Walter is an even greater problem than Griselda. Today we would call him obsessed. The narrator protests at his cruelty, and this, together with Chaucer's humanization of the tale, his greater 'realism', it is claimed, make Walter's monstrous actions and Griselda's improbable obedience all the more implausible.[66]

Moreover, at the end of the tale, Chaucer adds a warning to husbands not to test their wives hoping to find Griseldas because they will certainly fail.

Besides these two extremes, Chaucer includes other tales that illustrate how some marriages are shallow or loveless. The merchant tells a tale of a crude, loveless marriage between an old man, January, and a young woman, May. January takes his sexual pleasures with May, but within days after the wedding the squire, Damian and May plan a meeting for sex. None of the characters elicits sympathy. In his essay "Chaucer's *Merchant's Tale*," J.S.P. Tatlock says that January is a senile lecher and calls Damian a "paper doll." Tatlock says that sympathy for May "was averted by making May not worse than January but hardly a person at all."[67]

Additional Tales of Marriage

The shipman tells another tale of a shallow, loveless marriage in which money holds a higher place than loyalty and love. The merchant, preoccupied with his business, neglects his wife's needs for intimacy, and she is preoccupied with clothes. Money is borrowed twice and paid twice with sex. In his essay "The *Canterbury Tales* II: Comedy," Derek Pearsall says:

> But sex comes to the rescue again, and she pays her husband in the same coin as she paid the monk. So the hundred francs has gone the rounds, and so has the wife, and no-one seems much the worse for the experience. In fact, there is hardly a ripple on the surface of suburban life. There is a good deal of insight in this tale into the power of money, and the nature of sex as a commodity.[68]

Chaucer presents compromises between the all-or-nothing positions of the wife of Bath and the clerk. For example, in "The Nun's Priest's Tale," chickens portray a marriage that combines a wife's submission with her control over her mate. Pertelope is loyal and submits to Chanticleer's affections. Yet when they quarrel over Chanticleer's excessive worry about his dream, she readily scolds him, saying,

> How dare you say for shame, and to your love,
> That there was anything at all you feared?
> Have you no manly heart to match your beard?
> And can a dream reduce you to such terror?[69]

Chanticleer, in turn, prides himself by outwitting his wife with scholarly knowledge about dreams. In *The Art of the*

"*Canterbury Tales*," Paul G. Ruggiers says, "They have had their quarrel or debate, but their relationship is a happy and natural one elevated by the poet through the language of love."[70]

Similarly, the franklin tells a tale that portrays a respectful relationship in marriage. The knight Arveragus and the lady Dorigen make a marriage contract in which he promises that he will never assume mastery over her nor control her with jealousy, and she promises to be humble and faithful. Their marriage survives a challenging test because both husband and wife uphold the marriage contract. With this tale, Chaucer solves the problem of competition in marriage. Ruggiers says:

> His [Chaucer's] usual sanity now offers a common-sense solution to the bitter extremes posed by the Wife of Bath's *Prologue* and by the *Clerk's Tale*. The relationship of lovers in the matrimonial bond is that of mutually tolerant, trusting friends, neither of whom acquires mastery over the other. . . . Patience, endurance, temperance, self-control, discretion, self-knowledge are infinitely to be preferred to highhandedness in human relations, as Arveragus the wise man knows. The result is a marriage of the ideal sort.[71]

Thus, Chaucer uses *The Canterbury Tales* to present a variety of marriages that exist in this pilgrimage of life and offers a new idea that departs from the medieval norm.

The Nature of Human Faults

Another obvious theme in *The Canterbury Tales* is the imperfections displayed by people in medieval England. On one hand, Chaucer identifies human foolishness, innocuous faults that make people look silly and cause embarrassment but no serious harm. On the other hand, Chaucer explores moral failings in people whose behavior causes pain or harm to others. For the most part, Chaucer takes a humane and forgiving attitude toward wrongdoers, even though he treats particular faults with bitter irony. John Gardner describes Chaucer as an observer of human foibles: "He had a critical eye, as all his poetry proves. No fault in man or woman could escape him. But he was more amused than judgmental. He enjoyed his green medieval world and all its citizens."[72] He is nonjudgmental in that he seldom states a moral opinion; instead, he

A tavern keeper pours wine for a customer. Excess is one of many human faults featured in The Canterbury Tales.

provides details and uses language that allows the reader to draw the moral conclusion about a character.

Chaucer provides details in the prologue and the tales that the reader would conclude make characters seem foolish. In particular, several characters look foolish because they are gullible. For example, the carpenter, John, in "The Miller's Tale" seems foolish because he believes Nicholas's claim that a flood is coming. Chanticleer, in "The Nun's Priest's Tale," has just been warned of a fox in a dream, but he proves susceptible to the fox's flattery and is captured as a result. The fox, for all his slyness, proves equally gullible.

Chaucer describes other characters who are simply foolish because of their excesses. The summoner, Chaucer says, "wore a garland set upon his head/Large as the holly-bush upon a stake/Outside the ale-house,"[73] creating the image of a foolish drunk. Sometimes the excesses are harmless, as in the case of the prioress's excessive sentimentality. Chaucer says that she wept if she saw a mouse in a trap, that she fed her dogs with the finest food from her table, and "bitterly she wept if one [of her dogs] were dead/Or someone took a stick and made it smart;/She was all sentiment and tender heart."[74] In medieval times, certainly, weeping over a dead mouse or feeding a dog at the table would have seemed silly. Perhaps the most outrageous character is Chaucer's knight Topaz, who seems hardly in touch with reality. Brewer describes Chaucer's depiction: "The knight's love-longing without a lady, the riding out into Fairyland, fighting a giant, ceremonially putting on his armour, sleeping in it in the open, all delightfully absurd."[75]

Chaucer usually treats the foolishness of his characters with jolly good humor, but he also criticizes those who are morally corrupt. From the details that Chaucer provides and the language he uses, it is apparent that he disapproves of cheating and greed. He points out how both the miller on the pilgrimage and the miller in "The Reeve's Tale" cheat their customers by overweighing their grain or taking some of it. The merchant in "The Shipman's Tale" neglects his wife to count his money, and the canon in "The Canon's Yeoman's Tale" charges money for fake lessons in alchemy.

Chaucer, however, treats those who do violence toward others more harshly. The judge in "The Physician's Tale" is portrayed as shockingly cruel for plotting to take Virginia from her family to serve his sexual pleasure. Also cruel are the two mothers-in-law in "The Man of Law's Tale," who set Constance adrift to prevent her marriage to their sons. In this tale, the absence of detail recording the time at sea allows the reader to imagine this young woman's ordeal.

Chaucer also provides details and selects harsh words for the church officials involved in corruption, such as greed, hypocrisy, neglect of duties, and sexual impropriety. For example, the friar seems to feel no guilt in taking money from the poor and arranging marriages for a fee, which he uses to buy alcohol for himself. The monk neglects his simple, cloistered life of prayers and study and instead hunts and attires himself in fur and gold. With harsh words, Chaucer portrays the summoner's revolting appearance and sexual impropriety: He scares children and sells his mistress for a quart of wine. Chaucer paints the most critical picture of the pardoner. In "The Prologue," Chaucer portrays him as bug-eyed and

Unlike the pious friar pictured here, Chaucer's friar is morally corrupt. He takes money from the poor to buy alcohol and neglects his religious duties.

effeminate, although he notes that he is a good preacher. It is the pardoner's hypocrisy that Chaucer portrays most vividly. The first part of his tale is one of the sermons he preaches in church, effectively railing against sin. But then the pardoner openly advertises his fake relics and invites parishioners to give him money.

Though details in the tales make clear what sorts of behavior Chaucer finds objectionable, others also clarify behavior he considers moral. He describes the clerk, the plowman, and the parson in positive terms. For example, the clerk wears worn clothing and devotes his time to study, indicating that he does not pursue money and luxury. Like Chaucer himself, he likes books. Similarly, the plowman and the parson, who are brothers, are honest, hardworking men. The plowman pays his taxes and finds peace in a simple life. The parson, the only church official on the pilgrimage who is not corrupt, lives a good life so as to lead his parishioners by example. Like the clerk, the parson is poor in worldly goods but rich in spirituality. Chaucer places his tale at the end of the book and makes it a serious sermon about Christian theology.

Throughout his life Chaucer defended one value—charity, the inclination to find some decency in even the most wretched men—and he most vehemently attacked one vice repeatedly—self-righteousness. Gardner says that Chaucer's theme never changes; it is that "God is love, and so is man at his best, whether he proves it in bed or singing at the altar; and evil is non-love, the fear, pride, concupiscence [lust], bigotry, or high doctrine that lead a man to think about no one but himself, forgetting the cornerstone of Christian faith."[76]

Notes

Introduction: *The Canterbury Tales:* Chaucer's "Plenty"

1. Velma Bourgeois Richmond, *Geoffrey Chaucer.* New York: Continuum, 1992, p. 198.

2. Quoted in Piero Boitani and Jill Mann, eds., *The Cambridge Chaucer Companion.* Cambridge, UK: Cambridge University Press, 1986, p. 106.

3. Bernard F. Huppe, *A Reading of the "Canterbury Tales."* Albany: State University of New York, 1964, p. 241.

4. Quoted in Bernard D. Grebanier et al., eds., *English Literature and Its Backgrounds,* vol. 1, rev. ed. New York: Dryden, 1949, p. 721.

Chapter 1: The Life of Geoffrey Chaucer

5. Quoted in John Gardner, *The Life and Times of Chaucer.* New York: Vintage Books, 1977, p. 62.

6. Donald R. Howard, *Chaucer: His Life, His Works, His World.* New York: E.P. Dutton, 1987, p. 12.

7. Gardner, *The Life and Times of Chaucer,* p. 62.

8. Derek Brewer, *A New Introduction to Chaucer,* 2nd ed. New York: Longman, 1998, p. 16.

9. Gardner, *The Life and Times of Chaucer,* p. 19.

10. Howard, *Chaucer,* p. 53.

11. Howard, *Chaucer,* p. 4.

12. Gardner, *The Life and Times of Chaucer,* p. 143.

13. Howard, *Chaucer,* p. 95.

14. Brewer, *A New Introduction to Chaucer,* p. 117.

15. Howard, *Chaucer,* p. 196.

16. Gardner, *The Life and Times of Chaucer,* p. 197.

17. Howard, *Chaucer,* p. 187.

18. Howard, *Chaucer*, p. 199.

19. Gardner, *The Life and Times of Chaucer*, p. 205.

20. Howard, *Chaucer*, p. 214.

21. Howard, *Chaucer*, p. 457.

22. Gardner, *The Life and Times of Chaucer*, p. 279.

23. Quoted in Gardner, *The Life and Times of Chaucer*, p. 314.

24. Gardner, *The Life and Times of Chaucer*, p. 3.

Chapter 2: Historical Background

25. T. Walter Wallbank and Alastair M. Taylor, *Civilization Past and Present*, vol. 1, rev. ed. Chicago: Scott, Foresman, 1949, p. 346.

26. Grebanier et al., *English Literature and Its Background*, p. 75.

27. Grebanier et al., *English Literature and Its Background*, p. 60.

28. Will Durant, *The Reformation: A History of European Civilization from Wyclif to Calvin: 1300–1564*, vol. 6. New York: Simon and Schuster, 1957, p. 40.

29. Gardner, *The Life and Times of Chaucer*, pp. 56–59.

Chapter 3: The Cast of Characters

30. Howard, *Chaucer*, p. 410.

31. Kemp Malone, *Chapters on Chaucer*. Baltimore: Johns Hopkins, 1951, p. 181.

32. Howard, *Chaucer*, p. 412.

33. Malone, *Chapters on Chaucer*, p. 203.

34. Geoffrey Chaucer, *The Canterbury Tales*, trans. Nevill Coghill. New York: Penguin, 1977, p. 31.

35. Chaucer, *The Canterbury Tales*, p. 32.

36. Malone, *Chapters on Chaucer*, p. 173.

37. Howard, *Chaucer*, p. 10.

38. Howard, *Chaucer*, p. 416.

39. Quoted in Don Nardo, ed., *Readings on "The Canterbury Tales"*. San Diego: Greenhaven Press, 1997, p. 171.

Chapter 4: The Plots

40. Richmond, *Geoffrey Chaucer*, p. 103.

41. Trevor Whittock, *A Reading of the "Canterbury Tales."* Cambridge, UK: Cambridge University Press, 1968, p. 185.

42. Whittock, *A Reading of the "Canterbury Tales,"* p. 127.

43. Huppe, *A Reading of the "Canterbury Tales,"* p. 138.

44. R.M. Lumiansky, *Of Sondry Folk: The Dramatic Principle in the "Canterbury Tales."* Austin: University of Texas Press, 1955, p. 156.

45. Richmond, *Geoffrey Chaucer*, p. 78.

46. C. David Benson, *Chaucer's Drama of Style: Poetic Variety and Contrast in the "Canterbury Tales."* Chapel Hill: University of North Carolina Press, 1986, p. 143.

47. Whittock, *A Reading of the "Canterbury Tales,"* p. 262.

48. Richmond, *Geoffrey Chaucer*, p. 118.

49. Huppe, *A Reading of the "Canterbury Tales,"* p. 240.

Chapter 5: Literary Devices and Themes

50. Quoted in Boitani and Mann, *The Cambridge Chaucer Companion*, p. 14.

51. Malone, *Chapters on Chaucer*, p. 195.

52. Quoted in Boitani and Mann, *The Cambridge Chaucer Companion*, p. 186.

53. Quoted in Richard J. Schoeck and Jerome Taylor, eds., *Chaucer Criticism: "The Canterbury Tales,"* vol. 1. Notre Dame, IN: University of Notre Dame Press, 1960, p. 35.

54. Chaucer, *The Canterbury Tales*, p. 504.

55. Malone, *Chapters on Chaucer*, p. 193.

56. Chaucer, *The Canterbury Tales*, p. 103.

57. Chaucer, *The Canterbury Tales*, p. 186.

58. Chaucer, *The Canterbury Tales*, p. 124.

59. Chaucer, *The Canterbury Tales*, p. 298.

60. Chaucer, *The Canterbury Tales*, p. 231.

61. Quoted in Boitani and Mann, *The Cambridge Chaucer Companion*, p. 190.

62. Chaucer, *The Canterbury Tales*, p. 244.

63. Quoted in Schoeck and Taylor, *Chaucer Criticism*, p. 26.

64. Quoted in Boitani and Mann, *The Cambridge Chaucer Companion*, pp. 156–57.

65. Brewer, *A New Introduction to Chaucer*, p. 300.

66. Quoted in Boitani and Mann, *The Cambridge Chaucer Companion*, p. 156.

67. Quoted in Schoeck and Taylor, *Chaucer Criticism*, pp. 178–79.

68. Quoted in Boitani and Mann, *The Cambridge Chaucer Companion*, p. 136.

69. Chaucer, *The Canterbury Tales*, p. 235.

70. Paul G. Ruggiers, *The Art of the "Canterbury Tales."* Madison: University of Wisconsin Press, 1965, p. 190.

71. Ruggiers, *The Art of the "Canterbury Tales,"* pp. 229–30.

72. Gardner, *The Life and Times of Chaucer*, pp. 18–19.

73. Chaucer, *The Canterbury Tales*, pp. 36–37.

74. Chaucer, *The Canterbury Tales*, p. 23.

75. Brewer, *A New Introduction to Chaucer*, p. 363.

76. Gardner, *The Life and Times of Chaucer*, p. 310.

For Further Exploration

Below are some suggestions for essays on *The Canterbury Tales.*

1. From "The Prologue," pick the three pilgrims who stand out in your mind as 1) the most amusing, 2) the most likeable, and 3) the most unattractive. Describe the pilgrim generally and state specifically the features that made you chose him or her for each category. *See* Kemp Malone, *Chapters on Chaucer.* Baltimore: Johns Hopkins, 1951.

2. Analyze the personality and role of the host. Read what Chaucer says in "The Prologue," the sections between tales, and the prologues to upcoming tales for information on the host. How would you evaluate him in terms of courtesy, leadership, and entertainment? Cite examples to support your analysis. *See* Kemp Malone, *Chapters on Chaucer.* Baltimore: Johns Hopkins, 1951; R.M. Lumiansky, *Of Sondry Folk: The Dramatic Principle in the "Canterbury Tales."* Austin: University of Texas Press, 1955.

3. The wife of Bath and the clerk portray opposite views of marriage in their tales. On what specific issues do they differ? Can you find any hints in their tales that indicate what Chaucer's opinion might be? Cite lines or details from the tales to support your analysis. *See* George Lyman Kittredge, "Chaucer's Discussion of Marriage," in *Chaucer Criticism: The Canterbury Tales,* ed. Richard J. Schoeck and Jerome Taylor. Notre Dame, IN: University of Notre Dame Press, 1960; Trevor Whittock, *A Reading of the "Canterbury Tales."* Cambridge, UK: Cambridge University Press, 1968.

4. Chaucer has been described as "nonjudgmental," yet he clearly offers opinions concerning immoral behavior. Explain what technique Chaucer uses that allows him to be nonjudgmental and at the same time offer opinions on morality. Select two immoral characters and explain first how they are immoral, according to Chaucer, and then cite lines from the tale or tales to support your choices. *See* Derek Brewer, *A New Introduction to Chaucer,* 2nd ed. New York: Longman, 1998; Bernard F. Huppe, *A Reading of the "Canterbury Tales."* Albany: State University of New York, 1964.

5. Of the tales of the miller, the reeve, and the shipman, which one do you think would most appeal to an uneducated audience, and which one would be the most successful for an oral reading? Explain your selections using lines from the tale or tales to support your choice. *See* Don Nardo, ed., *Readings on "The Canterbury*

Tales." San Diego: Greenhaven Press, 1997; Velma Bourgeois Richmond, *Geoffrey Chaucer.* New York: Continuum, 1992.

6. Chaucer's tales portray corruption as well as goodness. Identify the nature of corruption in the merchant's, the pardoner's, and the canon's yeoman's tales. In which tale is the corruption most extreme? Explain the reasons for your selection. *See* Derek Brewer, *A New Introduction to Chaucer,* 2nd ed. New York: Longman, 1998; Bernard F. Huppe, *A Reading of the "Canterbury Tales."* Albany: State University of New York, 1964.

7. Read Chaucer's "Tale of Sir Topaz," a tale in which Chaucer skillfully writes bad poetry to create a parody and satire. What specific elements in the style and content make the tale bad poetry? What does Chaucer satirize? *See* Derek Brewer, *A New Introduction to Chaucer,* 2nd ed. New York: Longman, 1998; C. David Benson, *Chaucer's Drama of Style: Poetic Variety and Contrast in the "Canterbury Tales."* Chapel Hill: University of North Carolina Press, 1986.

8. Three tales portray the use of magic—the prioress's, the squire's, and the franklin's. How does magic contribute to the plot of each tale? In which tale do you think Chaucer has made the most clever or imaginative use of magic? Explain why you chose the tale you did. *See* Derek Brewer, *A New Introduction to Chaucer,* 2nd ed. New York: Longman, 1998; R.M. Lumiansky, *Of Sondry Folk: The Dramatic Principle in the "Canterbury Tales."* Austin: University of Texas Press, 1955.

9. The tales of the friar and the summoner are paired, with each figure being the main character of the other's tale. Explain 1) how Chaucer describes the friar and the summoner in "The Prologue," 2) how they get into conflict following the wife of Bath's prologue, and 3) how each makes a fool of the other in the tales. *See* Robert Worth Frank Jr., "The *Canterbury Tales* II: Comedy," in *Chaucer Criticism: "The Canterbury Tales,"* ed. Richard J. Schoeck and Jerome Taylor. Notre Dame, IN: University of Notre Dame Press, 1960; R.M. Lumiansky, *Of Sondry Folk: The Dramatic Principle in the "Canterbury Tales."* Austin: University of Texas Press, 1955.

10. Identify the elements that make "The Knight's Tale" a romance. How does the tale reflect real life during the Middle Ages? What elements of the tale represent exaggeration and fantasy designed for entertainment or satire? See C. David Benson, *Chaucer's*

Drama of Style: Poetic Variety and Contrast in the "Canterbury Tales." Chapel Hill: University of North Carolina Press, 1986; William Frost, "An Interpretation of Chaucer's *Knight's Tale*," in *Chaucer Criticism: "The Canterbury Tales,"* ed. Richard J. Schoeck and Jerome Taylor. Notre Dame, IN: University of Notre Dame Press, 1960.

11. Three tales—the clerk's, the physician's, and the man of law's—portray female characters who suffer at the hands of someone else. Identify 1) how each suffers, 2) who imposes the suffering and why, and 3) how the suffering ends. Place the women in rank order according to who suffers the most injustice to who suffers the least. Explain your ranking. *See* C. David Benson, *Chaucer's Drama of Style: Poetic Variety and Contrast in the "Canterbury Tales."* Chapel Hill: University of North Carolina Press, 1986; Trevor Whittock, *A Reading of the "Canterbury Tales."* Cambridge, UK: Cambridge University Press, 1968.

12. *The Canterbury Tales* is described as a metaphor for the journey of life. How does "The Parson's Tale" support this idea? How does this tale differ from all of the others? Why do you think scholars believe that Chaucer intended to place this tale last? See Derek Brewer, *A New Introduction to the Chaucer,* 2nd ed. New York: Longman, 1998; Trevor Whittock, *A Reading of the "Canterbury Tales,"* Cambridge, UK: Cambridge University Press, 1968.

13. What functions are served by Chaucer's use of multiple voices in *The Canterbury Tales?* (See chapter 5.) *See also* E. Talbot Donaldson, "Chaucer the Pilgrim," in *Chaucer Criticism: "The Canterbury Tales,"* ed. Richard J. Schoeck and Jerome Taylor. Notre Dame, IN: University of Notre Dame Press, 1960; Paul G. Ruggiers, *The Art of the "Canterbury Tales."* Madison: University of Wisconsin Press, 1965.

14. How did Chaucer create a new style and form for *The Canterbury Tales?* What in his reading and travels contributed to the style and content? What opportunities at court offered him encouragement? *See* Derek Brewer, ed., *Geoffrey Chaucer.* Athens: Ohio University Press, 1974; John Gardner, *The Life and Times of Chaucer.* New York: Vintage Books, 1977.

Appendix of Criticism

Chaucer Is England's First Great Poet

Geoffrey Chaucer produced what English had lacked since Anglo-Saxon times—literary creations worthy to rank with the best works of contemporary European literature. This he did, not by trying to eschew all foreign influence, but by steeping himself in French and Italian literature and profiting by what he learned from them; and he was great enough to learn by experience. In his early work, such as *The Boke of the Duchesse* (1370), *The Hous of Fame* (c. 1380), *The Parlement of Foules* (c. 1382), he was restricted by the conventions of French poetry, such as the use of a dream leading into an allegory. But already his very active career had brought him into contacts with all kinds of men—first as the son of a London vintner, then as page and official in noble and royal households, followed by embassies to Italy and an important post in the customs; and this had already given him the insight into character which is so important an element of his power. In *Troilus and Criseyde* he transmutes the conventional figures of Boccaccio's voluptuous story into subtle and moving character studies. His later posts as clerk of the king's works, surveyor of roads, and sub-forester gave him further experience of life; and his mature experience was contained in his last and greatest work, the incomplete *Canterbury Tales*. In this the framework of a pilgrimage was a stroke of genius, for it gave him full scope for his gifts. Chaucer had his limitations; he lacked the profundity of a Dante or the spiritual vision of a Bunyan. But his breadth of sympathy and understanding of character, his tolerance and humour, his powers of construction and description, his sense of drama and of vivid imagery, all combine to make him one of the greatest writers in the English language. He was the first Englishman who was a man of the world and created poetry out of what he saw around him. Moreover, his mastery of dramatic characterization was something new in English literature; Criseyde is in many ways the first real character of English fiction. Unlike some great writers, his worth was immediately recognized; and for almost a century every courtly writer of English poetry acknowledged Chaucer and [poet John] Gower as his masters, and strove to imitate their methods.

A.R. Myers, *England in the Late Middle Ages*.
New York: Penquin, 1982.

Chaucer's Canterbury Tales Launches the English Renaissance

A tremendous knowledge of the times can be gleaned from the works of this genius. In addition to the brilliance of humor and poetical description which have made the *Canterbury Tales* immortal, the reader learns of religious attitudes of the day, the sources from which Chaucer derived his plots, the prevailing belief in astrology, witchcraft, and relics, and the language of the period. But first and foremost Chaucer deserves fame as a brilliant storyteller.

Chaucer's use of the Midland dialect helped make it the language of future English literature, just as Dante's use of the Tuscan dialect fixed the Italian tongue. Secondly, Chaucer's use of "high comedy" has never been surpassed. He is always satirizing, but his humor and irony are gentle and sympathetic. Thirdly, because his humor does not preach and because he took such a wholehearted pleasure in the everyday realities of this life, Chaucer stands as a great forerunner of the English Renaissance. If Petrarch and Boccaccio are looked upon as poets of the Italian Renaissance, Chaucer may be regarded as occupying a similar position in the English Renaissance.

> Alastair M. Taylor and T. Walter Wallbank, *Civilization Past and Present*. New York: Scott, Foresman, 1949.

The Prologue Identifies the Medieval Social Order

In introducing the pilgrims Chaucer arranged them so that we can see their relationships and remember them more easily. The Knight rides with his son and a servant or retainer, the Prioress with another nun and three priests, the London Guildsmen with their wives and hired cook, the crooked Pardoner with his cohort the Summoner. The Sergeant of Law and the Franklin, both great purchasers of land, ride together. Others are described *as if* they rode together: Prioress, Monk, and Friar; Clerk and Merchant; Manciple, Reeve, and Miller; Shipman, Physician, and Wife. The Miller rides colorfully in front, tooting his bagpipe; the Reeve, the Miller's enemy, and a suspicious man by nature, rides last.

In this description Chaucer embedded an old-fashioned ideal of social harmony, "the Three Estates." It was thought society consisted of knights, clergy, and commons, "those who fight, those who pray, and those who work." Gower in his *Confessio* began with an explicit statement of this ideal, but Chaucer only included an ideal member of each Estate: the Knight (described as a crusader), the Parson (a self-sacrificing parish priest), and his "brother" the Plowman (who "lived in peace and perfect charity"). The Clerk seems idealized too, though as a student he has not yet defined his place in adult life—he is described in terms of what he does not have or want, what he would like, and so on. The largest number of pilgrims are of the "commons," which reflects the social circumstances of the day: the commons were now stratified into intermediate classes extending up to the rich and powerful, like the Man of Law or the Franklin, and down to the poor and marginal, like the drunken Cook.

Chaucer arranged these groups in a sequence from high to low, divided symmetrically by the ideal portraits. First are the Knight and his small retinue, the Prioress and hers, and the Monk and Friar; next the Merchant, introducing members of the "middle" and merchant class; and last the "churls," introduced first in a lump (lines 542–544), among whom Chaucer wryly includes himself.

> Donald R. Howard, *Chaucer: His Life, His Works,*
> *His World.* New York: E.P Dutton, 1987.

Chaucer Attacks Richard II's Absolutism in Two Tales

Watching court affairs from the quiet and seclusion of Greenwich, far from "the stremës hed," and talking with friends during his visits to London, Chaucer observed with increasing disappointment the growth of his beloved king's absolutist theory, and at last he was stirred to make his sentiments known in the most effective way available to him as an admired court poet. He began his great revision. He tore out the Man of Law's tale of Melibeus and inserted, instead, the Man of Law's tale of Custance, or Constancy, an intentionally overstated argument for blind submission to authority (to God, to king, to husband)—precisely what King Richard was demanding. The heroine's meek response to her father's order that she go marry a sultan far, far from home, is typical:

"Alias! unto the Barbre nacioun [*barbarian*]
I moste anoon, syn that it is youre willë
But Crist, that starf for our redempcioun [*died*]
So yeve me grace his heestës to fulfillë!
I, wrecchë woman, no fors though I spillë! [*die*]
Wommen are born to thraldom and penancë,
And to been under mannës governancë."

Even standing alone, this pious, carefully tongue-in-cheek tale—a work not comic but ironic—must have struck the knowing in Chaucer's audience as tactful criticism of some of King Richard's most cherished opinions. But to remove all doubts, Chaucer followed the *Man of Law's Tale* with a new tale for the Wife of Bath (she had been, in his earlier draft, the teller of the *Shipman's Tale*). Whereas formerly the Wife was simply the jovial revealer of women's wiles, she now becomes a bold advocate of the rights of women, beginning her remarks with a frontal attack on the lawyer's oppressive ideal, Constancy:

"Experiencë, though noon auctoritee
Were in this world, is right ynogh for me
To speke of wo that is in mariagë!"

Thus Chaucer's tactfully indirect series on right and wrong government, that is, the "marriage group," was born.

He had never written more brilliantly. The colloquial lilt is as
human as ever, the imagery as luminous, the plotting as economical
and sure. And Chaucer's development of his overall theme is equally
brilliant. The Wife of Bath's argument is essentially a noble and self-
less one, that a wife (or subject) should be given control, whereupon
she will inevitably relinquish government to her lord out of love. But
the argument she offers has also its darker implications, for she claims
that if a wife is *not* freely granted control she will seize it and tyran-
nize her lord. That argument sets the medieval hierarchy on its head.

John Gardner, *The Life and Times of Chaucer.*
New York: RandomHouse, 1978.

Chaucer Inherits His Middle English Language

Chaucer's language *was* Middle English, the lineal descendant of Old
English or Anglo-Saxon. The truth is that Chaucer inherited a particular English style, which he enriched by his borrowings from French
and Italian and Latin.

All poets need a prepared language and an accepted tradition to begin
to write in, or they could not begin at all; a poet's stock-in-trade is
words, not 'life' or 'feelings' or 'ideas'. A medieval poet was particularly
dependent on a formed verbal tradition; he needed it to help himself,
and also to fulfil that other essential demand of the rhetoric of poetry,
to communicate with the audience. No poet could stand up in his pulpit before the audience, as medieval poets did,1 if he was not prepared
to use a poetic language with which his audience was reasonably familiar, and which it could be expected to understand and even to like.

Derek Brewer, *Chaucer: The Poet as Storyteller.*
London: Macmillan, 1984.

Chaucer Advances the Middle English Language

Until nearly the end of the century French was still the language of the
upper classes, and facility in it was a necessary accomplishment for all
who wished to move, or be thought to move, in polished society. In
the latter half of the century, however, English was ousting its rival.
John of Trevisa, writing in 1385, ascribed this to the effect of the Black
Death, which killed off or frightened away many of the old teachers

99

and caused a break in tradition; but the anti-French prejudices engendered by the Hundred Years War probably had their effect as well. In 1362 English was made the language of the law-courts, and next year, for the first time, the chancellor opened Parliament in English. The city of London issued a proclamation in English in 1384 and the earliest known will in English dates from 1387. It is significant that Henry of Lancaster spoke in English instead of French when he formally claimed the throne in 1399, and [poet John] Gower and Chaucer had already begun to write in English. Henceforth the teaching of French waned in importance, and by the late fifteenth century even ambassadors to France were sometimes ignorant of the language. At the same time ability to read and write English grew steadily in the upper and middle classes. If education had still been limited to ecclesiastics, this development would have been much slower; for the language of the Church and its schools was Latin, and English was of interest to it only for homiletic [preaching in sermons] and didactic purposes.

Once teachers had begun to take account of English, a great difficulty confronted them. During the two hundred and fifty years in which it had been merely the patois of the lower classes (except, perhaps, in the remote parts of the north and west, where the gentry also may have spoken the language) it had had no social or literary conventions to preserve a standard English, and existed only in many dialects. Which of these should be used as the standard tongue? It may seem natural to us that the victorious dialect should have been that of the east midlands, the region in which London and the two universities were situated, and in which the king most frequently held his court. But the very presence of the court and the universities, centres of the use of French and Latin, meant that the east midland dialect had become the most degraded and poverty-stricken of all. Its eventual victory was due partly to the prestige of the man who used it at the end of the fourteenth century—the poet Chaucer.

A.R. Myers, England in the Late
Middle Ages. New York: Penguin, 1982.

The Printing Press Makes *The Canterbury Tales* Available to Readers

A revolutionary influence in religion and education was the art of printing, which made it possible to multiply books with a speed, an accuracy, and a cheapness hitherto inconceivable. Yet this revolutionary technique, discovered in Germany about 1450, was introduced into England by a man of thoroughly conventional outlook. William Caxton (?1422–1491) was no humanist, and not even a professional scrivener [a professional copyist]. When he set up his printing press in 1476 in the precincts of Westminster Abbey he was a successful mercer with literary tastes, who had picked up the idea of printing while living in Flanders. Caxton's patrons were important persons—Edward IV, Earl Rivers, the Earl of Arundel; but neither they nor the growing literate public, avid for more reading-matter than manuscript methods of production could supply, were Renaissance scholars. The few Englishmen who wanted the Latin or Greek classics could get them from French or Italian presses. Hence Caxton devoted himself almost entirely to translating and publishing in English a wide range of books likely to appeal to his conservative public. Most of his books were therefore didactic or religious, the biggest and most popular of them being the *Golden Legend,* a compendium of Saints' lives which had been a favourite for nearly three centuries; but he also published works of Chaucer.

A.R Myers, *England in the Late Middle Ages.* New York: Penquin, 1982.

Elizabethan Poets and Critics Misunderstood Chaucer's Middle-English Rhythm

Between Chaucer's time and Shakespeare's, the pronunciation of English changed, so much so that Chaucer's poems no longer sounded right. He was admired for his rhetoric and his "philosophy," his skill as a storyteller, and as the "first finder of our fair language," but his rhythms were a puzzle and his rhymes did not sound true. People tolerated Chaucer's "rough" verses and assumed he had a tin ear. Henry Peacham, writing in 1622, found "under a bitter and rough rind," a kernel of "conceit and sweet invention." [Poet John] Dryden said there was in his verse "the rude sweetness of a Scotch tune"—"natural and pleasing, though not perfect."

Because Chaucer satirized certain corruptions of medieval religion, Elizabethans thought of him as a sort of proto-Protestant; then, thinking this, they attributed to him old poems on religious subjects that couldn't possibly have come from his pen. [Poet John] Milton always refers to "our Chaucer," praising him as the originator of the English poetic tradition; but his favorite tale was the " Plowman's Tale," an alliterative poem not by Chaucer at all, and it sounds as if he hadn't read *Troilus* or the Knight's Tale, or even (strangely) the Clerk's Tale.

A few writers in the sixteenth and seventeenth centuries insisted Chaucer's meter was regular. In the eighteenth century certain men of letters proposed that one could reconstruct the pronunciation of fourteenth-century English. [Poet] Thomas Gray, writing about 1760, suggested that if the final *-e* in Chaucer, and some *e*'s within words, were pronounced, it would make his verses scan. And he was right. Not only different pronunciations but a different system of rhythm had existed in Chaucer's time. The old system disappeared during the lifetime of Sir Thomas Wyatt (1503–1542), whose editor, Tottel, "smoothed out" his old-fashioned rhythms.

Donald R. Howrad, *Chaucer: His Life, His Works, His World*. New York: E.P. Dutton, 1987.

Chaucer Ranks with Dante as the Greatest Medieval Poet

In the fourteenth century, which witnessed clearly both a decay of the medieval and a promise of the Renaissance, the honors in literature were divided fairly between the Italians and the English; and, indeed, the honors in Renaissance art and literature were to be divided in similar fashion. If Italy produced her Dante and her Petrarch and her Boccaccio, England produced her Chaucer and her Piers Plowman Poet and her Pearl Poet. Chaucer looms more and more, as time goes by, a greater figure than Petrarch or Boccaccio and a formidable rival of Dante and the medieval mystics. Which of the two titans, Chaucer or Dante, by our twentieth-century standards is the more characteristically medieval? Probably Dante. Which is the greater poet as poet? Again, probably Dante. Which is the more comprehensive interpreter of humanity and critic of life? Unquestionably Chaucer.

George K. Anderson and Robert Warnock, *The World in Literature*. New York: Scott, Foresman, 1950.

Chaucer's Pilgrims Are "God's Plenty"

He must have been a man of a most wonderful comprehensive nature, because, as it has been truly observed of him, he has taken into the compass of his Canterbury Tales the various manners and humors (as we now call them) of the whole English nation, in his age. Not a single character has escaped him. All his pilgrims are severally distinguished from each other; and not only in their inclinations but in their very physiognomies and persons. Baptista Porta [a famous Italian physiognomist, or one who judges human character from facial features] could not have described their natures better, than by the marks which the poet gives them. The matter and manner of their tales, and of their telling, are so suited to their different educations, humors, and callings, that each of them would be improper in any other mouth. Even the grave and serious characters are distinguished by their several sorts of gravity: their discourses are such as belong to their age, their calling, and their breeding; such as are becoming of them, and of them only. Some of his persons are vicious, and some virtuous; some are unlearned, or (as Chaucer calls them) lewd, and some are learned. Even the ribaldry of the low characters is different:

the Reeve, the Miller, and the Cook, are several men, and distinguished from each other as much as the mincing Lady-Prioress and the broad-speaking, gap-toothed Wife of Bath. But enough of this; there is such a variety of game springing up before me, that I am distracted in my choice, and know not which to follow. 'Tis sufficient to say, according to the proverb, that here is God's plenty.

> Bernard D. Grebanier, Samuel Middlebrook,
> Stith Thompson, and William Watt. *English Literature and Its Background*. New York: Dryden, 1951.

The Man of Law's Tale Is Criticized as a Structureless Romance

The *Knight's Tale* is a complete and perfect version of a medieval romance, worked out with all the resources of Chaucer's literary study and reflexion; tested and considered and corrected in every possible way. The story of *Constance* (the *Man of Law's Tale*) is an earlier work in which almost everything is lacking that is found in the mere workmanship of the *Knight's Tale;* though not, of course, the humanity, the pathos, of Chaucer. The story of *Constance* appears to have been taken by Chaucer from one of the least artificial specimens of medieval romance, the kind of romance that worked up in a random sort of way the careless sequence of incidents in a popular traditional tale. Just as the tellers of the stories in [Scottish poet J.F.] Campbell's *Highland Tales,* and other authentic collections, make no scruple about proportion where their memory happens to fail them or their irrelevant fancy to distract them, but go on easily, dropping out a symmetrical adventure here and there, and repeating a favourite "machine" if necessary or unnecessary; so the story of *Constance* forgets and repeats itself. The voice is the voice of Chaucer, and so are the thoughts, but the order or disorder of the story is that of the old wives' tales when the old wives are drowsy. All the principal situations occur twice over; twice the heroine is persecuted by a wicked mother-in-law, twice sent adrift in a rudderless boat, twice rescued from a churl, and so on. In this story the poetry of Chaucer appears as something almost independent of the structure of the plot; there has been no such process of design and reconstruction as in the *Knight's Tale.*

> W.P. Ker, *Epic and Romance: Essays on Medieval Literature*. New York: Dover, 1957.

The Host's Role Turned Upside Down

In literature, and on the stage, the normal relationships of life may be, and often are, turned topsy-turvy for humorous purposes. The technique here used is that of broad comedy, with a deliberate and complete disregard for the realities of social intercourse.

The device which makes it possible for the host to behave as he does is explained in detail in the general prolog. Chaucer's account is humorous from start to finish, the host telling the pilgrims what to do and the pilgrims obeying his orders in comic reversal of the customary relationship between an innkeeper and his guests. The host begins by using a little flattery before bringing forward his proposal. . . .

Having opened the way by these words, he makes his proposal, presenting it as an inspiration which has just come to him. . . .

This is the proposal. You will note that the host does not say what his scheme is. He merely assures the pilgrims that it will give them pleasure. And now he asks them to take a vote on it. . . .

What are they to vote for? Not for any particular scheme, since no scheme has been laid before them. In effect, they are asked to sign a blank cheque. They must agree to do what the host tells them to do. And the agreement must be unanimous. Moreover, this action must be taken at once, and without any discussion whatsoever. Such a proposal seems a bit unreasonable, but the pilgrims accept it without demur, as they well might on an imaginary pilgrimage done in comic style, though hardly on a pilgrimage in real life. . . .

The host now outlines his scheme for keeping the pilgrims occupied on the way to Canterbury and back. . . .

The scheme is obviously preposterous. Picture in your mind's eye thirty-odd pilgrims on horseback, strung out for a quarter of a mile on the Canterbury road, trying to listen to one of their number who is telling a tale as they ride along. How well could they hear him? Those nearest to the teller of the tale might hear much of it, though even they would miss a good deal. The rest of the pilgrims (by far the greatest number) would hear nothing, or, at most, would hear the speaker's voice without being able to make out the words. But did any of the pilgrims point out this practical difficulty, when the host made his proposal? Not at all; they took it without a murmur. They also accepted the host as their guide and governor, and made no objection to the huge fine which anyone who withstood him was to pay.

Kemp Malone, *Chapters on Chaucer.*
Baltimore: Johns Hopkins, 1951.

Concrete Details Give Life to the Fabliaux

The vivid concrete detail with which his *fabliaux* are scattered carries Chaucer's realistic style to its most intense degree. We learn the precise type of window in *The Miller's Tale*, we see the chink through which the moon shines in *The Reeve's Tale*, the Merchant counting his money and the wife in her garden in *The Shipman's Tale*, the convenient bough in *The Merchant's Tale;* we see the Friar in *The Summoner's Tale* drive away the cat from the warmest place on the bench. It is this characteristically realistic style, combined with the fantastically indecent plots, that leads to the blunt use of coarse words, which is shocking but at the same time emotionally releasing (provided, that is, that it is not a device so frequently used that it suffers the law of diminishing returns and gives a coarse, undiscriminating tone to the style). Outstandingly indecent are *queynt* (with the actions of Nicholas piling Pelion on Ossa) and *swyve*, while *pisse, toute ers, fert* (all concrete Anglo-Saxon words with no French elegance, distance or abstraction), together with the notions they are used to convey, are all more than sufficiently gross.

Not only physical objects but people are in many cases described, as they are in the *General Prologue*, with sharply vivid detail, the most notable being Alison in *The Miller's Tale*, who is so bright and clean, with her black embroidery on her collar, her white smock, huge brooch, laced legs, and breath as sweet as old apples in hay. Simkin the Miller of *The Reeve's Tale* is brought clearly before us, especially with his shiny bald head, while a number of others, less fully noted, have still their bright detail, like the gay Yeoman's appearance with short green cloak of the fiend in *The Friar's Tale* or the handsome Monk's smart newly shaven tonsure [head] in *The Shipman's Tale*.

Events themselves are described in the same vivid way, the best example being the gloriously farcical fight in the bedroom at the end of *The Reeve's Tale*.

Alan has slept with the Miller's daughter to their mutual satisfaction. When dawn approaches, having said an affectionate good-bye, he creeps back to his own bed. There to his astonishment he finds two people, for his friend John has tricked the Miller's wife into the bed, (thinking it her own) where they have had 'a merry fit'. So Alan gets into the other bed and crudely tells John (as he thinks) what he has been up to. But of course he tells the girl's father, the Miller, who arises with a roar of rage to take vengeance. He catches Alan by the throat. Alan punches him on the nose so that the blood streams. They fall and rise and fall on the other two sleepers. The wife, believing herself in bed with her husband, thinks it is the two clerks who are fighting, but her actual companion John knows better. Each springs up to join the fray, with different motives; he to help his friend, she, as a good housewife, to beat down either or both of the guests.

It is a wonderful conclusion that she gives her own husband a fearful crack on his white bald skull. While in one sense it is all too good to be true, the events are nevertheless described with concrete precision and accuracy of causal explanation, in a remarkably transparent and apparently objective style, which is extremely naturalistic and convincing. The things and deeds seem to shine through the words. We do not think of style in the passage just quoted—we are too eagerly watching the fun. Nor do we engage with the personalities in these poems, even when we are on their side. We do not see into their minds. We are detached from the individual persons because we live imaginatively in the situation as a whole.

Derek Brewer, *Chaucer: The Poet as Storyteller.*
London: Macmillan, 1984.

Chaucer Uses Reduction to Create Humor

The basic technique of the satirist is reduction: the degradation or devaluation of the victim by reducing his stature and dignity. This may be done on the level of plot and will almost always be continued to the level of style and language.

To be reduced to a type is a less fearful circumstance than to be reduced to an animal, madman or machine, but it is unpleasant enough. It implies, if less rigorously, that the type-figure can never step out of the role imposed on him, or act in freedom. Although satire uses it too, typing is the essential device in stage comedy and ironic humour. Chaucer in the *Canterbury Tales* classifies his pilgrims according to the humours [body fluids thought to determine a person's disposition] and by physiognomy [judging characters from facial features], an ancient lore which combined the humours with astrology and medicine. The Wife of Bath looks and believes as she does because of her horoscope: the planets at her birth imposed a pattern of character on it, which explains her dress, boldness, erotic adventurousness and love of travel. It does not matter whether Chaucer believed in this kind of explanation: he used it to extract exquisite comedy out of the types he created.

Matthew Hodgart, *Satire.*
New York: McGraw-Hill, 1969.

Red and White Symbolize Perfection and Unity

Readers with even passing acquaintance with medieval iconography [traditional symbolism] are, no doubt, familiar with the tandem use of the colors white and red as a pictorial convention, for in both England and on the continent the conjoining of these two colors is a symbolic staple in the literature of the chivalric knight, the courtly lover, the Virgin Mary, saints in general, the mystic, and even the alchemist. . . .

The relatively early tale of St. Cecilia, later ascribed to the Second Nun, provides an excellent example of such imagery. As a sign of the state of blessedness achieved by both Cecilia and Valerian, an angel appears with two crowns "of roses and of lilie." . . .

White and red together are, then, the result of an act of completion or perfection, and it should be noted that Cecilia, for all her purity, does not achieve her apotheosis [exalted to divine rank] with the dual crowns until she has a mate, a complement, who can love her with "clene love" (VIII, 159) rather than love "in vileynye" (VIII, 156). The same symbolism is, in effect, in the description of the daughter of Virginius in the *Physician's Tale*. . . . The daisy in the *Legend of Good Women* is presented as a creation of Dame Nature, brought to perfection or excellence through the use of white and red. . . .

In regard to the symbolic colors, Virginia is an ideal, that which "should be." Moreover, like the daisy and St. Cecilia, Virginia is that which is *made* perfect, and that perfection is clearly created by a balance or unity among her dynamic attributes. . . .

A final and perhaps most interesting example of Chaucer's use of white and red may be found in the life of a third saintly figure, Custance of the *Man of Law's Tale*. As the Sowdanesse contemplates the effect of her son's proposed conversion and marriage to Custance, the Sowdanesse first mocks the sacrament of Baptism:

'Coold water shal nat greve us but a lite!' (II, 352),

and then continues her mockery by employing familiar imagery:

'For thogh his wyf be cristned never so white,
She shal have nede to wasshe awey the rede
Thogh she a font-ful water with hire lede' (II, 355–57)

The Sowdanesse proposes to let the red dominate the white or, in other words, to create an imbalance or disharmony in the natural ordering of the colors. Yet the "whiteness" of Custance is not washed over by the blood of the slaughter, and in imagery clearly intended as a counterpoint to the Sowdanesse's mockery, Custance prays in language borrowed from the Good Friday address to the Cross. . . .

The juxtaposition of white and red, then, forms the figure of the Lamb, a meditative symbol of unity and harmony.

Julian N. Wasserman and Robert J. Blanch, eds., *Chaucer in the Eighties.* Syracuse, NY: Syracuse University Press, 1986.

Chaucer Adds "Context" to the Borrowed Tales

The whole conception of the *Canterbury Tales* as a collection of stories within the framework of the tale-telling on the pilgrimage to Canterbury is the most ambitious instance of Chaucer's inclination throughout his artistic career to re-interpret received materials by setting them within 'frames' of various forms, 'frames' which through Chaucer's structural devising enable the received story to be read within a context constructed to extend and give super-added meaning to the borrowed story-shape. . . .

Apart from Chaucer's distinctive use of prologues in the framework to the *Tales*, he also develops comparable structural techniques within the construction of some of the tales themselves, as with the tales of the Physician, Merchant, and Pardoner. Part of the creative process in structuring such tales involves Chaucer's conjoining of his narration of some pre-existing story with an ample and thematically important first phase or preface, so that the received story can be re-interpreted within a new context. In the *Physician's Tale* the story—of how the Roman father kills his beloved young daughter rather than allow her to be dishonoured by a corrupt judge—is provided in Chaucer's new structural disposition with an opening discourse on the balance between nature and nurture and on the upbringing of children. . . .

Similarly in the *Canon's Yeoman's Tale*, the lengthy first 'Part' is a hectic account of the processes of alchemy, followed in the second 'Part' by the narrative of the tale itself, which stands in pointed juxtaposition with this technical first 'movement' of the Yeoman's utterance as a whole.

Even more striking as a comparable structural disposition is the way Chaucer develops the opening phase of the *Merchant's Tale*. Before the narrative begins to fulfil its fabliau pattern, Chaucer has introduced the lengthy prefatory discourse of well over a hundred lines ('To take a wyf it is a glorious thyng . . . ': 1268ff), enumerating the joys and by implication the sorrows of marriage. . . .

In the *Nun's Priest's Tale*, Chaucer's version of the fable of the cock and fox, the cockerel's prescient dream of his fate prompts a discourse and dispute on the truth of dreams which is almost a third of the length of the whole tale, so that the narrative of the tricking of the cock does not get under way until sometime past the mid-point of the tale (3187ff). This virtuoso 'preface' of prejudiced argument and anecdotage so establishes the question of predestination that the unfolding story-pattern of the familiar fable cannot but be seen in relation to what has gone before. . . .

When Chaucer's structural technique in using his sources and analogues is examined, it becomes clear that there is no paradox in the fact that Chaucer invents so few stories yet is so inventive a story-teller. Chaucer's inventiveness will often consist in an 'art of context', of creating a structure which enables an interaction between materials which Chaucer has had the perceptiveness to bring together. In this sense Chaucer's most innovative wielding of structure lies in his technique of 'contextualizing' received materials.

Piero Boitani and Jill Mann, eds., *The Cambridge Chaucer Companion*. Cambridge, UK: Cambridge University Press, 1986.

The Magical Horse in "The Squire's Tales"

Perhaps the most impressive mechanical/magical device in the *Canterbury Tales* is the flying "hors of bras" [brass horse] which a visiting ambassador . . . gives to the Mongol king Cambyuskan as one of four apparently magical gifts in the *Squire's Tale;* the other gifts are a mirror that can reveal distant and/or secret events, a ring that gives knowledge of the language of birds and of herbal lore, and a sword that can heal as well as wound. Although we know of no specific source for the tale as a whole, such magical toys are commonplace in medieval romances. . . . What is most interesting about Chaucer's version of the flying horse is its distinctly mechanical nature: in order to make it go, the rider must "trille a pyn, stant in his ere" [twirl a peg within his ear]; when it comes time to land, one must "bidde hym descende, and trille another pyn" [bid him descend and twirl another pin]. A third "pyn" causes the horse to "vanysshe anoon/Out of the sighte of every maner wight" [vanish completely from all men's sight]; whether that vanishing is to be interpreted as magical or mechanical is unclear. . . .

Even more interesting than the horse of brass itself, however, is the reaction Chaucer ascribes to the courtiers and common people who come to stare at this marvel in the courtyard: to them it seems "a fairye," a fairy or magical thing, even though it is obviously mechanical, an attitude which seems to suggest that the essence of its magic could be that no one quite understands how it works. No one, we are told, could make the horse move at all, even though the courtiers employ such mundane mechanical devices as windlasses and pulleys: "And cause why?" the Squire asks. "For they ken nat [had not] the craft," he answers.

But even if no one knows precisely how the "magic" horse works, everyone expresses an idea about what kind of magic or technology is entailed here. . . . Some think it is another Pegasus [a flying horse in an ancient Greek myth]; others fear it is a replica of the Trojan horse and has armed warriors inside it. Still others assume it is made by "som magyk,/As jogelours pleyen." . . . We should note that "magyk" is here attributed to jugglers, whose craft is comprised of sleight-of-hand and technical illusion, not to manipulators of supernatural or demonic powers.

Don Nardo, ed., *Readings on "The Canterbury Tales."* San Diego: Greenhaven Press, 1997.

A Hen's Attempted Murder?

Chaucer's Nun's Priest's Tale is well known as a morality tale as well as a glimpse of life in fourteenth-century England. Various commentaries on this tale have focused on the morals presented, made comparisons of this fable with those told by Aesop, concentrated on the rooster Chanticleer's dream, the use of courtly verse, and Chaucer's apparent reference to the Peasant's Revolt of 1381. However, no one has addressed the idea that it may be relating a possible murder attempt. In light of the poisonous nature of some of the herbs she prescribed for him, and the fact that she discouraged him from heeding his warning dream, I will address the concept that the portrayal of the hen, Pertelote, recommending medical treatment for her husband/rooster, may indeed represent a murder attempt.

Robin J. Kennedy, "Why Attempted She My Mordre?":
Pertelote vs. Chanticleer. www. umich.edu.

Chaucer's Respect for Humanity

Critics have generally praised in the Chaucer of the *Tales* the power to show, not simply people doing things for good or evil, but what those people and their actions are really like, so that their personalities become more vital and individual and life-enriching than those of many people whom we know intimately. Certainly he is the poet with an eye for those essences that make a woman a particular woman or even a rooster a particular rooster; and he is justly acclaimed for his healthy humanity, his joy in people and actions as they are—not ideally powerful, beautiful, or wise, impotent, ugly, or stupid, good or evil, but fascinating particular creations which, if we are big enough men, we contemplate dispassionately and at the same time with gratitude and gusto.

A. Kent Hieatt and Constance Hieatt, eds., *The Canterbury Tales by Geoffrey Chaucer.* New York: Bantam, 1982.

The Ideal of Feminized Masculinity

The *Canterbury Tales* lacks male heroes in the sense of central figures in the narrative, but it is not entirely lacking in examples of admirable male behaviour, as we have already seen in Arveragus, Aurelius, Alla, Melibee. It is however the figure of Theseus in the *Knight's Tale* that represents the fullest development of an ideal of feminised masculinity. Displaced as he is from the hero's central position by the younger knights Palamon and Arcite (whose pairing debars each of them likewise from a central heroic role), it is nevertheless to Theseus that it falls to voice and to embody the values that constitute the wisest response to their experiences. And the key element in these values is the womanly quality of pity.

At the opening of the tale Theseus, antagonist and conqueror of 'Femenye', the Amazonian land of women, seems to represent a mas-

110

culinity sharply opposed to women and womanliness. But the conquest culminates not in enslavement, but in a marriage; it is the *separateness* of 'Femenye', its severance from the masculine world that is resisted; the marriage of Theseus and Hippolyta signals its reintegration. Even more important, the marriage symbolises the union of masculinity and femininity in each partner. Hippolyta is 'The faire, hardy queene of Scithia' (882); her physical bravery is not rejected as 'unwomanly', but is as admirable as her beauty. And in Theseus, as the first scene of the narrative action makes clear, masculine prowess is infused with feminine 'pitee'. As he returns to Athens to celebrate his victory and his wedding, he is confronted by a double line of kneeling women, wailing and begging for his pity. . . .

'Pitee renneth soone in gentil herte' is an oft-repeated maxim in Chaucer's poetry, and it is applied to Theseus in the scene where he and his retinue come upon Palamon and Arcite fighting in the grove. Theseus's first response to the discovery of their identities is angrily to condemn them to death, but he is persuaded to forgive them by the intercessory pleas of the queen and all the ladies with her.

> Jill Mann, *Geoffrey Chaucer.* Atlantic Highlands,
> NJ: Humanities Press International, 1991.

Chaucer's Tales of Pathos

The narratives we may call 'tales of pathos' [tales arousing the feelings of pity, sympathy, tenderness or sorrow]—the tales of the Man of Law, Clerk, Physician, Prioress and Monk—make greater demands on a modern reader's historical sense and imaginative sympathies than probably any other grouping in the *Canterbury Tales.* . . .

'Tales of pathos', however, are not a genre. No two narratives are the same: they include a saint's life, a miracle of the Virgin, a series of *de casibus* stories, a religious romance, an expanded exemplum, and a tale. These tales vary, too, in the degree of pathos aimed for and achieved. The *Second Nun's Tale* and the *Monk's Tale*—with one striking exception—are only marginally pathetic, whereas the *Clerk's Tale,* the *Prioress's* and the *Man of Law's* are intensely so. . . .

Unlike so many of Chaucer's narratives, they are in no way comic. Chaucerian irony is also absent. There is little or no complexity. Characters are generally one- or two-dimensional, motivated by a single virtue: constancy, patience, simple piety. The treatment of scene tends to be abstract. The action is played on a bare stage, so to speak. The narratives concentrate on crucial incident, moments of extreme threat, pain, distress, anguish. Or, if there is a happy ending, tearful bliss.

Chaucer's principal artistic concern (with the *Monk's Tale,* again, possibly an exception) is to produce a strong emotional effect. The situations—death of a child, separation of loved ones, being set adrift at sea, martyrdom—in themselves arouse feeling. Special attention is given to the emotional reaction of the central character, and, often, of witnesses, and of the narrator as well.

> Piero Boitani and Jill Mann, eds., *The Cambridge Chaucer Companion.* Cambridge, UK: Cambridge University Press, 1986.

The Parson Becomes Intercessor for the Pilgrims

The Parson replaces the Host ultimately as docent because this is the function of a priest, not an innkeeper, and all the pilgrims to Canterbury in becoming pilgrims to the Heavenly Jerusalem must take the *wey* or *via* of Penitence. . . . And so it does not seem an exaggeration to say that the destination of the pilgrimage becomes, by the interlocked metaphorical and dramatic structure, not so much the Canterbury shrine as the Parson's Tale, because it unfolds the *wey* to Him who is the way, the truth, and the light. We have noticed that the Parson has been silenced before this, not allowed to speak. The theology is sound in this respect. The economy of grace, and the form of the fiction, dictate that the assent to the Parson's priestly and metaphorical solicitation be voluntary, that there be a cooperation on the part of the pilgrims with grace. The "heer" of the Shipman's denial in the Epilogue of the *Man of Law's Tale,* "heer schal he nat preche;/He schal no gospel glosen here ne teche." [II (B) 1179–80], was right, dramatically, structurally, and "morally." An appearance there would have been crassly inopportune from a structural consideration. The last place is and must be reserved for the Parson, for he plays the intercessory and ecclesiastical role at the end, the most vital spot in the work. . . .

From such considerations as these, habitual, reflexive to the mediaeval person, we can say that it was indeed advisable for Chaucer to end upon some virtuous or holy business. Likewise it was seemly to give that member of the group who was best qualified to speak at the end of the Tales, "space and audience" in order that he might counsel the pilgrims to predispose them for that end which is potentially, always, the *now* for the Christian. If the pilgrims could forget themselves, under the hearty encouragings of the Host, so far as to "pleye by the weye," then it behooved the Parson, the professional admonisher and mediator, to recall them to the realization that the *weye* was a *via,* that play had to be remedied by a Christian work, that *fable* had to give place to *morality,* that the readiness is all; that death is precarious for the Christian not so much in its inevitability as in its unexpectedness, because the state of grace must be maintained up to and at the moment of death. The Parson becomes, supremely, the Pastor in the actual as well as the parabolic [as in a parable] sense. And he does it with a gently insistent humor that is not mealy-mouthed.

Richard J. Schoeck and Jerome Taylor, eds., *Chaucer Criticism: "The Canterbury Tales."* Vol 1. Notre Came, IN: University of Notre Dame Press, 1978.

The Meaning of Chaucer's Retractions

In *The Retractation* Chaucer abandons all his roles except that of a sincere writer or translator of religious works in English. He is still a writer, his most enduring role. . . .

The Retractation is in many respects a fitting close to *The Canterbury Tales*. From the purely narrative point of view it provides a surprise for which, we can now see by hindsight, as in the *dénoument* of a detective story (the archetype of plots) some clues have previously been given, both in Chaucer's life and works, and in the sections of *The Tales* immediately preceding *The Retractation*. It has strong verbal and psychological links with *The Parson's Tale* and *The Manciple's Tale*. Within the structure of the pilgrimage it is much better, though less realistic, than what could only have been the anticlimax of a 'soper at oure aller coste' (I, 799). How could Chaucer, of all poets, with his *blasé* courtier's disdain even for a 'kynges feeste', have represented with any effectiveness the much more humble supper of this motley band of pilgrims in an inn? In a wider sense *The Retractation* reaches a conclusion that allows *The Canterbury Tales* to image the curve of a whole life, as so much narrative does. It represents an end to a lifelong quest, a kind of death. But that death was not for Chaucer a final end, a snuffing out of a pointless life, as it must be for so many modern readers. It represents a closure in this world, but a firm hope, by its very nature as assertion with repentance, of continuing what has always been, if not always recognised as such, the ultimate end of all the seeking, questions, questioning; the heavenly Jerusalem, where all things shall be made plain in glory, an ultimate closure that also means eternal life. . . .

Chaucer has had his turn and takes his leave, his immortality lying not in his works, even the religious ones, but elsewhere, in himself.

Derek Brewer, *A New Introduction to Chaucer*. London: Longman, 1998.

113

Chronology

1327
Edward III ascends the English throne.

1337
Outbreak of the Hundred Years' War between England and France.

1341?
Geoffrey Chaucer is born in London.

1346
The English defeat the French at Crécy.

1348–1349
The bubonic plague, known as the Black Death, sweeps through England, killing thousands.

1349
Chaucer begins his formal schooling at St. Paul's grammar school in London under headmaster William Ravenstone.

1356
The English are victorious at Poitiers; France's King John is captured and held under house arrest in London.

1357
Chaucer begins his education as a courtier when he is appointed to be a page in the household of Lionel, earl of Ulster, second son of Edward III.

1359–1360
Chaucer fights as a soldier against the French during the Hundred Years' War; he is taken prisoner during the siege of Reims but is ransomed soon after.

1360
Edward III and King John sign the Treaty of Bretigny, temporarily halting hostilities between England and France.

1360–1366
Few records exist, but sometime during this period Chaucer studies law and finance at the Inns of Court.

1366
Chaucer marries Philippa Roet, a lady-in-waiting to Queen Philippa; Chaucer's father dies.

1366–1367
Chaucer, now in the service of King Edward III as a civil servant and diplomat, receives a lifetime annuity from the king; Chaucer is sent to Milan; Duchess Blanche, wife of Edward III's son John of Gaunt, dies; Chaucer begins *The Book of the Duchess;* Prince Lionel dies.

1369
War with France resumes.

1371
Chaucer's friend John of Gaunt marries Constance, heiress of Castile and León; Gaunt had already taken Chaucer's sister-in-law Katherine as his mistress.

1372
Philippa Chaucer receives a lifetime annuity from John of Gaunt.

1372–1373
Chaucer travels to Italy, first negotiating the use of an English port by a Genoese merchant fleet and then arranging loans in Florence; the trip introduces him to Renaissance Italy and to the works of Dante, Boccaccio, and Petrarch, who later influence his writing.

1374
The king awards Chaucer a pitcher of wine a day for life as a reward for the success of the Italian mission; the Chaucers move to the gate-house at Aldgate; Chaucer is made controller of the king's custom and subsidy of wools, hides, and wool fells in the port of London; John of Gaunt grants Chaucer an additional annuity.

1376
Edward, the Black Prince, son of Edward III, dies.

1376–1377
Chaucer travels to the European continent three times for negotiations for peace and a prospective wife for Richard, Edward III's grandson.

1377
Edward III dies and Richard is crowned king; King Richard confirms Chaucer's annuities and duties.

1378
Chaucer travels to Italy and probably at this time acquires manuscripts of the works by Boccaccio and Petrarch, which he later uses in his poems.

1380
Chaucer completes *Parliament of Fowls.*

1381

Chaucer's mother dies; his son Lewis is born; peasants in Kent begin a revolt that spreads.

1381–1386

Chaucer works on *Troilus and Criseyde,* based on the Greek legend of the Trojan War; he begins a poem on Palamon and Arcite, later to become "The Knight's Tale."

1382

Richard marries Anne of Bohemia; Chaucer is given new responsibilities in addition to his controller job.

1385

Chaucer is appointed justice of the peace in Kent; he moves to Greenwich.

1386

Chaucer begins *Legend of Good Women;* Chaucer sits in Parliament for one session; Chaucer ends service at the customs and moves from the gatehouse over Aldgate; Chaucer writes phase one of *The Canterbury Tales:* the prologue and the knight's, miller's, and reeve's tales and perhaps the man of law's tale.

1387

Chaucer's wife, Philippa, dies; Chaucer goes on a diplomatic mission to France.

1389

Chaucer is appointed clerk of the works, in charge of maintaining the Tower of London and royal properties.

1389–1393

Chaucer writes phase two of *The Canterbury Tales:* the marriage tales and the shipman's and nun's priest's tales.

1390

Chaucer is appointed to a royal commission for the repair of walls and ditches after a storm or flood; he is robbed and assaulted in this job.

1391

Chaucer resigns his commission; he is appointed deputy forester of the royal forest of North Petherton.

1392–1393

Chaucer writes the *Treatise on the Astrolabe* for his son, Lewis.

1393–1399
Chaucer writes phase three of the *Tales:* the tales of the pardoner, second nun, canon's yeoman, manciple, and parson, adding his retractations.

1394
Queen Anne and Constance both die.

1396
John of Gaunt marries Chaucer's sister-in-law Katherine, his mistress of more than twenty years.

1399
John of Gaunt dies; Richard is deposed by Henry of Bolingbroke, who ascends the throne as Henry IV.

1400
A conspiracy to restore Richard II to the throne fails; Richard is murdered while under arrest; Chaucer dies and is buried in London's Westminster Abbey, initiating what will become the famous Poet's Corner.

Works Consulted

Major Editions of *The Canterbury Tales*

Geoffrey Chaucer, *The Canterbury Tales.* Trans. Nevill Coghill. New York: Penguin, 1977.

———, *The Canterbury Tales.* Ed. F.E. Hill. London: Longmans, Green, 1935.

———, *The Canterbury Tales.* Ed. R.M. Lumiansky. New York: Simon and Schuster, 1948. Rev. trans. New York: Rinehart, 1954. The revised translation is a complete version in prose.

———, *Canterbury Tales.* Trans: J.U. Nicolson. New York: Garden City, 1934.

———, *The Canterbury Tales: A Selection.* Ed. Donald R. Howard and James Dean. New York: Signet, 1969.

———, *The Canterbury Tales Complete.* Ed. Robert A. Pratt. Boston: Houghton Mifflin, 1966. Middle English with extensive side notes.

A. Kent Hieatt and Constance Hieatt, eds., *The Canterbury Tales by Geoffrey Chaucer.* New York: Bantam, 1964.

J.M. Manley and Edith Rickert, *The Text of the Canterbury Tales.* 8 vols. Chicago: University of Chicago Press, 1940.

Theodore Morrison, ed., *The Portable Chaucer.* New York: Viking, 1949.

F.N. Robinson, ed., *The Works of Geoffrey Chaucer.* Boston: Houghton Mifflin, 1957. Middle English with textual notes.

Other Works by Chaucer

Albert C. Baugh, ed., *Chaucer's Major Poetry.* Englewood Cliffs, NJ: Prentice Hall, 1963.

John H. Fisher, ed., *The Complete Poetry and Prose of Geoffrey Chaucer.* New York: Holt, Rinehart, and Winston, 1977. Includes *Canterbury Tales, Troilus and Criseyde, Book of the Dead, Parliament of Fowls, House of Fame, Treatise on Astrolabe,* and *Equatorie of Planets.*

Biographies of the Author

Derek Brewer, *Chaucer in His Times.* London: Thomas Nelson, 1963. This book places Chaucer in his public work during the Middle Ages.

———, ed., *Geoffrey Chaucer.* Athens: Ohio University Press, 1974. A collection of essays explaining Chaucer's roles in the Middle Ages, especially good on how he was influenced by literature from many places and other times.

Marchette Chute, *Geoffrey Chaucer of England.* New York: E.P. Dutton, 1946. Focuses on Chaucer as a particularly English writer.

John Gardner, *The Life and Times of Chaucer.* New York: Vintage, 1977. A good source on Chaucer's public life in the royal court and the influence of his travels on his writing.

Donald R. Howard, *Chaucer: His Life, His Works, His World.* New York: E.P. Dutton, 1987. A thorough work covering Chaucer's personal life, his public life, and commentary on his major works.

Roger Sherman Lomis, *A Mirror of Chaucer's World.* Princeton, NJ: Princeton University Press, 1965. Portraits of Chaucer, books he read, his royal friends, and drawings of real nuns and illustrations of tales.

Derek Pearsall, *The Life of Geoffrey Chaucer: A Critical Biography.* Oxford, UK: Blackwell, 1992. This source places Chaucer's life in his time and provides critical commentary on his works.

Edward Wagenknect, *The Personality of Chaucer.* Norman: University of Oklahoma Press, 1968. This book focuses on the character, personality, beliefs, and humor of Chaucer.

Literary Criticism

C. David Benson, *Chaucer's Drama of Style: Poetic Variety and Contrast in the "Canterbury Tales."* Chapel Hill: University of North Carolina Press, 1986. An analysis of the way dramatic theory applies to the tales, Chaucer's narrative voice, and an analysis of the fabliau and religious tales.

Peiro Boitani and Jill Mann, eds., *The Cambridge Chaucer Companion.* Cambridge, UK: Cambridge University Press, 1986. A collection of essays on literary and social background, Chaucer's earlier works, and major kinds of tales, such as exemplum and romance.

Derek Brewer, *A New Introduction to Chaucer.* 2nd ed. New York: Longman, 1998. This work combines biographical information with social and historical information and summarizes and interprets Chaucer's major works.

Bertrand H. Bronson, *In Search of Chaucer.* Toronto: University of Toronto Press, 1963. This book is a collection of lectures, including one on the *Canterbury Tales* that explains how Chaucer worked and thought.

Helen Cooper, *Oxford Guides to Chaucer: "The Canterbury Tales."* Oxford UK: Oxford University Press, 1989. This work discusses each tale and provides information on sources, themes, genre, and style.

Norman Davis et al., comps., *A Chaucer Glossary.* Oxford, UK: Clarendon, 1979. A dictionary of Middle English words from Chaucer's works.

Margaret Hallissy, *A Companion to Chaucer's "Canterbury Tales."* Westport, CT: Greenwood, 1995. This source analyzes each tale separately, with brief summaries.

Edwin J. Howard, *Geoffrey Chaucer.* New York: Twayne, 1964. The author provides historical background, a Chaucer biography, chapters on *Troilus and Crisedye,* short analysis of the tales, and a Chaucer evaluation.

Bernard F. Huppe, *A Reading of the "Canterbury Tales."* Albany State University of New York, 1964. This book covers a few tales by theme: the prologue development, differing realities, marriage, corruption in the church, and overall structure.

Maurice Hussey, A.C., Spearing, and James Winny, *An Introduction to Chaucer.* Cambridge, UK: Cambridge University Press, 1965. This source provides information on Chaucer's relation to the church, his Middle English, and his broad knowledge as revealed in the tales.

William Witherle Lawrence, *Chaucer and the "Canterbury Tales."* New York: Columbia University Press, 1950. Lawrence discusses what is real and artificial, the sequence of tales, marriage, the endings, and the fabliaus.

R.M. Lumiansky, *Of Soundry Folk: The Dramatic Principle in the "Canterbury Tales."* Austin: University of Texas Press, 1955. This book takes each tale separately, treating it as a play performance.

Kemp Malone, *Chapters on Chaucer.* Baltimore: Johns Hopkins, 1951. About half of the book discusses Chaucer's earlier works, and four chapters cover the pilgrims, providing brief commentary on their tales.

Jill Mann, *Geoffrey Chaucer.* Atlantic Highlands, NJ: Humanities Press International, 1991. Mann discusses select characters and tales from a feminist point of view.

Don Nardo, ed., *Readings on "The Canterbury Tales."* San Diego: Greenhaven Press, 1997. A collection of essays covering the structure and language, major themes, and analysis of select tales.

Velma Bourgeois Richmond, *Geoffrey Chaucer.* New York: Continuum, 1992. Richmond organizes the tales by topic: structure, romances, religious and satiric tales, and sermons. Three chapters are included on Chaucer's earlier works.

Paul G. Ruggiers, *The Art of the "Canterbury Tales."* Madison: University of Wisconsin Press, 1965. This book divides tales into sections on comedy and romance and concentrates on styles and themes.

Richard J. Schoeck and Jerome Taylor, eds., *Chaucer Criticism: "The Canterbury Tales."* Vol. 1. Notre Dame, IN: University of Notre Dame Press, 1960. A collection of essays by Chaucer scholars on several major tales, on techniques, and on Chaucer's voice.

Trevor Whittock, *A Reading of the "Canterbury Tales."* Cambridge, UK: Cambridge University Press, 1968. Whittock discusses each tale separately and focuses on the literary qualities present in each.

Historical Background

Morris Bishop, *The Horizon Book of the Middle Ages.* New York: American Heritage, 1967. This work covers social history, such as knights, crusades, religion, towns, trades, and peasant labor.

Marc Bloch, *Feudal Society: Social Classes and Political Organization.* Vol. 2. Trans. L.A. Manyon. Chicago: University of Chicago Press, 1961. A good explanation of governance during the Middle Ages and how power was maintained.

Carole Lynn Corbin, *Knights.* New York: Franklin Watts, 1989. This book explains the training and equipment of knights, their place in castle life, and the importance of chivalry.

Will Durant, *The Reformation: A History of European Civilization from Wyclif to Calvin: 1300–1564.* Vol. 6. New York: Simon and Schuster, 1957. A general history explaining the main events and trends in politics, exploration, arts, religion, science, and individual countries in Europe.

Joseph and Frances Gies, *Life in a Medieval Castle.* New York: Thomas Y. Crowell, 1974. This source tells about the kinds of castle activities Chaucer would have been part of, such as hunting, holidays, and households staff jobs.

Bernard D. Grebanier et al., eds., *English Literature and Its Backgrounds.* Vol. 1. Rev. ed. New York: Dryden, 1949. A literature text with selections by major writers, plus sections providing historical and cultural background for each literary period.

F.E. Halliday, *Chaucer and His Worlds*. New York: Viking, 1968. A picture book of people and places in Chaucer's England, with some biographical information.

Gertrude Hartman, *Medievel Days and Ways*. New York: Macmillan, 1937. Hartman covers lords, vassals, knights, squires, pages, peasants, and the development of guilds, architecture, and printing.

Kathryn Hinds, *Life in the Middle Ages*. New York: Marshal Cavendish, 2001. Four books in this series are all color illustrated. *The Countryside* tells about the manor, rural villages, and farm life. *The Church* explains the men and women of the church establishment and holy days they celebrated. *The Castle* explains duties of the lord and lady, entertainment and festivals, and castle workers. *The City* explains homes and businesses inside the city walls, feast days, and how the plague affected the city.

A.R. Myers, *England in the Late Middle Ages*. New York: Penguin, 1952. A thorough social, political, economic, religious, and artistic history of Chaucer's time, when institutions of the Middle Ages were beginning to break down.

Mary R. Price, *Medieval Amusements*. Harlow UK: Longman, 1988. This book explains feasts and festivals, use of animals, plays, games, music, and dance.

Marjorie Reeves, *The Medieval Castle*. 2nd ed. Harlow, UK: Longman, 1988. This work explains how castles were built and protected.

Marjorie Rowling, *Everyday Life in Medieval Times*. New York: Dorset, 1968. Rowling explains the roles of women, monks, friars, scholars, doctors, artists, and scientists and tells about the feudal system.

J.R.R. Tolkien, trans., "Sir Gawain and the Green Knight," "Pearl," and "Sir Orfeo." Boston: Houghton Mifflin, 1975. Poems written by a contemporary of Chaucer's. This source includes an appendix with a glossary and verse forms of romances.

T. Walter Wallbank and Alastair M. Taylor, *Civilization Past and Present*. Vol. 1. Rev. ed. Chicago: Scott, Foresman, 1949. A highly readable text in Western civilization, covering events from prehistory to 1650.

Jay Williams, *Knights of the Crusades*. New York: American Heritage, 1962. This book explains the importance of crusades, a definition of the perfect knight, and what happens to knights when they get old.

Index

Picture Credits

About the Author

Clarice Swisher is a freelance writer and a former English teacher. She taught English in Minnesota for several years before devoting full time to writing. She is the author or editor of more than twenty books, including *The Glorious Revolution, Victorian England,* and *Understanding* The Scarlet Letter, published by Lucent Books, and *The History of Nations: England* and *Galileo,* published by Greenhaven Press. She lives in Saint Paul, Minnesota.